Local Governments' Financial Vulnerability

Local Governments' Financial Vulnerability presents a conceptual framework developed to examine how vulnerable local finances were before and in the immediate aftermath of the COVID-19 pandemic crisis by mapping and systematising its dimensions and sources.

The model is then applied to eight countries with different administrative models and traditions: Australia, Austria, Bosnia and Herzegovina, Germany, Italy, Portugal, Spain, and the United States. Comparative results reveal not only that COVID-19 impacts and policy tools had a lot of similarities across countries, but also that financial vulnerability has an inherently contingent nature in time and space and can lead to paradoxical outcomes. The book shows that the impact of the crisis on local governments' finances has been postponed and that financial vulnerability is expected to increase dramatically for a few years following the pandemic, especially in larger and richer municipalities which are traditionally more autonomous and less financially vulnerable. The authors provide timely insights and analytical tools that can be useful for both academic and public policy purposes, to further appreciate local governments' financial vulnerability, especially during crises.

This book is a valuable resource for practitioners and academics, as well as students of public policy, public management, financial management, and public accounting. Local governments can use the framework to better appreciate and manage their financial vulnerability, while oversight authorities can use it to help local governments become less financially vulnerable or, at least, more aware of their financial vulnerability. Financial institutions, advisors, and rating agencies may use this publication to refine or revise their models of credit risk assessment.

Emanuele Padovani is Associate Professor of Public Management & Accounting at the University of Bologna, Italy. He has done extensive research, consultancy, and advisory activities in Europe in the area of accounting and financial management, financial analysis, and performance measurement and management, applied to regional and local governments and their subsidiaries.

Eric Scorsone is Associate Professor of Regional and Local Policy at Michigan State University, USA. He has extensive experience as a research, educator, and practitioner in the area of local government finance and intergovernmental finance and regulation and is currently Director of Michigan State University Extension Center for Local Government Finance.

Silvia Iacuzzi is Assistant Professor of Business Administration and Accounting at the University of Udine, Italy. She has worked and taught in over 40 countries. Her research focuses on public sector accounting and management, looking at value creation, stakeholder engagement, and performance measurement and management, particularly for local government and healthcare organisations.

Simone Valle de Souza is Assistant Professor of Resource Economics and Policy at Michigan State University, USA. Her research expertise includes public policy analysis, statistical analysis, and economic analysis, having taught microeconomics of public policy at undergraduate and graduate levels for 10 years. She also serves as Deputy Director for the Centre for Local Government at the University of New England, Australia.

Routledge Research in Urban Politics and Policy

Local Governments' Financial Vulnerability

Analysing the Impact of the COVID-19 Pandemic

Edited by
Emanuele Padovani, Eric Scorsone, Silvia Iacuzzi, and Simone Valle de Souza

LONDON AND NEW YORK

First published 2022
by Routledge
4 Park Square, Milton Park, Abingdon, Oxon OX14 4RN

and by Routledge
605 Third Avenue, New York, NY 10158

Routledge is an imprint of the Taylor & Francis Group, an informa business

British Library Cataloguing-in-Publication Data
A catalogue record for this book is available from the British Library

Library of Congress Cataloging-in-Publication Data
Names: Padovani, Emanuele, editor. | Scorsone, Eric A. (Eric Anthony), editor. | Iacuzzi, Silvia, editor. | Valle de Souza, Simone, editor.
Title: Local governments' financial vulnerability : analysing the impact of the COVID-19 pandemic / edited by Emanuele Padovani, Eric Scorsone, Silvia Iacuzzi and Simone Valle de Souza.
Description: Abingdon, Oxon ; New York, NY : Routledge, 2022. | Series: Routledge research in urban politics and policy | Includes bibliographical references and index.
Identifiers: LCCN 2021055570 (print) | LCCN 2021055571 (ebook) | ISBN 9781032228099 (hardback) | ISBN 9781032228105 (paperback) | ISBN 9781003274278 (ebook)
Subjects: LCSH: Local government--Finance. | COVID-19 (Disease)--Economic aspects. | COVID-19 (Disease)--Political aspects. | Comparative government.
Classification: LCC JS78 .L66 2022 (print) | LCC JS78 (ebook) | DDC 320.8--dc23/eng/20211213
LC record available at https://lccn.loc.gov/2021055570
LC ebook record available at https://lccn.loc.gov/2021055571

ISBN: 978-1-032-22809-9 (hbk)
ISBN: 978-1-032-22810-5 (pbk)
ISBN: 978-1-003-27427-8 (ebk)

DOI: 10.4324/9781003274278

Typeset in Times NR MT Pro
by KnowledgeWorks Global Ltd.

Contents

Tables

Contributors

Isabel Alijarde Brusca, Professor of Financial Economics and Accounting, University of Zaragoza, Spain.

Robert Blöschl, Researcher, KDZ – Centre for Public Administration Research, Austria (up to September 2021).

Brian Dollery, Professor of Economics and Director of the Centre for Local Government, University of New England, Australia.

René Geissler, Professor of Public Administration, Technical University of Applied Sciences Wildau, Germany.

Susana Jorge, Associate Professor of Public Sector Accounting and Financial Business Accounting, Faculty of Economics, University of Coimbra, Portugal, and affiliated at the Research Centre in Political Science, Portugal.

Liliana Pimentel, Assistant Professor, Faculty of Economics, University of Coimbra, Portugal, and member of CeBER Centre for Business and Economics Research, Portugal.

Jelena Poljašević, Associate Professor of Accounting and Auditing, Faculty of Economics, University of Banja Luka, Bosnia and Herzegovina.

Thomas Prorok, Deputy Managing Director, KDZ – Centre for Public Administration Research, Austria.

Mary Schulz, Associate Director, Extension Center for Local Government, Finance and Policy, Michigan State University, USA.

Andrea Wallace, Lecturer, University of New England, Australia.

1 Introduction

Emanuele Padovani, Eric Scorsone,
Silvia Iacuzzi, and Simone Valle de Souza

This is a timely publication as transboundary crises such as COVID-19, which cut across geographical, sectorial, and policy boundaries, may have not only pressing but also long-lasting effects. The outburst of the COVID-19 pandemic was different from previous global crises, as it affected society overnight with the implementation of lockdown, containment, and social distancing measures, the first time in history that such policies are applied on such a large scale. Governments have been faced with difficult trade-offs given the health, economic, and social challenges. The COVID-19 crisis has shaken the world: Beyond the unprecedented loss of lives and human tragedy, it has caused the worst economic downturn since the world wars, it has unveiled areas where reform efforts are necessary, it has massively accelerated some pre-existing trends, and it has questioned how economies are run setting in motion waves of change with a wide range of possible trajectories.

Research is needed to look back at the experiences in 2020 and draw out important lessons from different countries not only at the national but also at the local level, where the institutions closest to citizens provide proximity services and support the local economy and the development of local communities. Local governments (LGs) are at the frontline of the crisis management and recovery: They have a direct impact on people's life as they influence the functioning of local economies, the delivery of national governments' policies and that of proximity services, such as public health, security, and education. During the COVID-19 crisis, they have been responsible for critical aspects of containment measures, health care, social services, economic development, and public investment. On the policy side, the last 30 years have been characterised first by a decentralisation and an increase in local autonomy, and, in a second instance, by recentralisation efforts cutting back local powers and resources while intensifying

DOI: 10.4324/9781003274278-1

upper-level control and supervision measures (Pollitt and Bouckaert, 2017). Thus, an important issue which should not be underestimated is the financial condition of such institutions, which can determine their ability to deal with the crisis. The financial vulnerability of LGs to global shocks needs, therefore, to be further explored to learn from what happened in 2020 and make LGs more financially resilient and readier to deal with similar sudden shocks.

Local government, transboundary crises, and financial vulnerability

Global shocks with their dynamic and chaotic nature tend to be a challenge to governments (Peters, 2011). Even more, transboundary crises, that cut across geographical, sectorial, and policy boundaries such as the COVID-19 pandemic, multiply the strengths of their impacts and make responses much more complex and wicked (Boin and Lodge, 2016). Such global events have attracted the attention of scholars particularly in the past ten years following the 2008 financial crisis.

However, the COVID-19 pandemic has been different in nature and impact. Given its multifaceted nature and unprecedented scale, comparisons with past crises, including the 2008 financial crisis, have significant limitations. COVID-19 is proving unique in its uncertainty and impact on all sectors and regions of the world. In contrast to the situation during that financial crisis (Davies, 2011), global Gross Domestic Product growth fell by 3.5% in 2020 because the COVID-19 crisis affected the real economy, not just financial markets (OECD, 2021). Yet, impacts and reactions to the global pandemic have been different across countries and jurisdictions within a country (Maher et al., 2020; Nemec and Špaček, 2020; OECD, 2020a). Moreover, the COVID-19 pandemic, beyond having a global reach with local patterns, has spread relatively fast, differently from the 2008 crisis, which first affected financial markets, then the real economy, and finally local public finances (Grossi and Cepiku, 2014). In other words, the 2008 crisis had a slow onset, while the 2020 crisis has had a sudden onset (Hochrainer, 2006), since it has generally affected local services overnight, in correspondence with the implementation of lockdown and social distancing measures. Further, according to several authors, it is not to be underestimated that the 2008 financial crisis and the subsequent austerity measures, depending on where and how they were implemented, may have weakened LGs' ability to face the 2020 crisis (Ahrens and Ferry, 2020; OECD, 2020a). All in all, at the end of 2020, governments faced a difficult trade-off: managing the economic recovery and mitigating the impact of a second wave of the virus (OECD, 2020a).

This underlines the temporal dimension that Pollitt (2008) considers crucial in many public policy and management problems. From his "time toolkit," the duration, path, window of opportunity, and perspective elements seem relevant to this analysis. The COVID-19 pandemic struck in the winter of 2020 and is still ongoing while this book is in print. We can, thus, safely understand and analyse only the onset and the immediate aftermath of a pandemic that is still unclear when and how it will end. We can now properly grasp only the consequences of the measures taken in the spring and the summer of 2020 in different countries. Hence, time and space play a crucial role in analysing the consequences of such a global event.

The COVID-19 pandemic offers an interesting case study because of its immediateness, its newness, its global reach, and its impact on the real economy. It caused the deepest global recession since the world wars with the need for government interventions in a wide range of areas such as social distancing measures, infrastructure lockdown, economic transfers to businesses and families, as well as in novel services offered to the community (Anessi-Pessina et al., 2020). While the recovery is expected to bring most of the world back to pre-pandemic GDP levels by the end of 2022 (OECD, 2021), the global economy remains below its pre-pandemic growth path and in many countries living standards by the end of 2022 will not be back to the level expected before the pandemic.

It is interesting to explore local reactions to the same crisis across countries because the magnitude of fiscal responses measured by their monetary value varies significantly across jurisdictions (Grossi et al., 2020) depending on the pandemic load and different fiscal conditions, institutional arrangements, and administrative traditions (Saliterer et al., 2017). Yet, the policy tools used by different countries have a lot of similarities (de Jong and Ho, 2020): Supplemental measures and special budgets for extra spending on public health and social programs, appropriations for unemployment and companies, tax reliefs for individuals, workers, households, and businesses, as well as loans, loan guarantees, and debt relief for specific industrial sectors were provided by many governments to buffer against the adverse economic and social impacts of the pandemic. Because of such measures, many countries, including those that had the strong fiscal discipline and sound budgetary balances before the crisis, anticipate a significant jump in the level of LGs' indebtedness. The latter may have been induced also by how the accounting information has been used to take action to face the pandemic (Padovani and Iacuzzi, 2021). Moreover, the COVID-19 crisis also brought to light existing inequalities, the potential to exacerbate these problems, areas where reform efforts are necessary, and the importance of interjurisdictional governance (Grossi et al., 2020). Besides growing debt concerns and the setbacks on anti-poverty and equity enhancing initiatives, other long-term concerns include the seeming irrelevancy of fiscal discipline in influencing the pandemic response and the hidden social costs in postponing the necessary responses to global concerns, such as social and climate change issues (de Jong and Ho, 2020). These problems have highlighted the crucial role of LGs in addressing unexpected impacts and reducing inequalities, while maintaining a healthy outlook and financial condition.

Commentators (Anessi-Pessina et al., 2020) highlight that governments should have embraced a strategic approach in allocating resources for counteracting the impact of the pandemic by pursuing a dual set of goals: On the one hand, spend effectively in the short run, making good use of looser budgetary rules, and extensive emergency funds; on the other hand, lay the foundations to recover from the mounting debt produced by higher spending and lower revenues. This has led to rising concerns about fiscal sustainability in the long run because immediate national responses focused primarily on short-term output measures instead of long-term impacts on people's livelihood and sustainable development (Hopper, 2020). Hence, it is also interesting to understand whether LGs' institutional and fiscal frameworks (Geissler et al., 2021) were changed in the immediate aftermath, allowing them to run deficits and build-up debt or whether central government increased transfers to them to concentrate all deficits and debt at the national level and take sole responsibility for debt management.

Financial crises have attracted the attention of scholars particularly following the 2008 global crisis, which has made it imperative to appreciate how LGs react to such events. However, even after the 2008 crisis, the literature on the public administration response to the global crisis has mainly focused on public policy issues (Peters, 2011; Meneguzzo, 2013), central government's effort to restore sound financial conditions (Grossi and Cepiku, 2014; Bracci et al., 2015), and crisis management (Hochrainer, 2006; Boin and Lodge, 2016). The concept of financial vulnerability has been mainly discussed in terms of financial condition and performance (Cabaleiro et al., 2013), while the issue of resilience, i.e. how LGs face and absorb external shocks, has not been addressed apart from a few notable exceptions (Barbera et al., 2017; Steccolini et al., 2017; Barbera et al., 2020). In their recent definition, Barbera et al. (2020, p. 533) claim that vulnerability is the "reduced capacity to cope with emerging shocks." Likewise, Arunachalam et al. (2017, p. 52) define as vulnerable a local council that, without some structural reform and major revenue and expense adjustments, "is highly unlikely to be able to manage unforeseen financial shocks and any adverse changes in its business and in general economic conditions."

Content of the book

Starting from a review of the relevant theoretical concepts, this manuscript considers the different understandings and perspectives of the financial vulnerability of LGs and develops a framework to analyse its multifaceted sources developing an analytical framework which takes into consideration both spatial contingencies, in terms of geography and sector and time dynamics, as far as the speed of the pandemic and the perspective of the analysis (before and immediate aftermath) are concerned. Chapter 2 proposes such a conceptual framework to appreciate how financially vulnerable LGs are before and in the immediate aftermath of a global pandemic crisis. The framework considers internal, external, and perceived sources of financial vulnerability, deriving different perspectives for analysis. Chapter 2 also explains the method of analysis applied in the selected countries.

In Chapters 3–10, the framework is then applied to eight OECD countries that were impacted differently by the Coronavirus (OECD, 2021), namely: Australia, Austria, Bosnia and Herzegovina, Germany, Italy, Portugal, Spain, and the United States. They have a different administrative tradition (Ongaro, 2008) and LG characteristics (Kuhlmann and Wollmann, 2014; Geissler et al., 2019; OECD/UCLG, 2019), so much that they epitomise diverse case studies (Seawright and Gerring, 2008). For each country, the main findings are discussed through the application of the proposed framework. This allows us to verify how the framework can be applied to different geographical contexts highlighting what were the institutional arrangements, administrative rules, revenue, and expenditure structures before the pandemic and how they were affected by the measures taken in the immediate aftermath of the crisis. In each of the eight countries, the analysis explores what conditions and what measures lead to an increase in financial vulnerability across LGs and which one favoured financial resilience.

In Chapter 11, the conclusion brings together and compares findings from single country analyses. Assessing findings from individual chapters reveals that while the impact of the crisis was highly asymmetric across and within countries, policy tools had a lot of similarities across countries but financial vulnerability has an inherent contingent nature in time and space that can lead to paradoxical outcomes. The main overall implications are twofold. On the one hand, they allow to review and refine the conceptual framework. On the other hand, the identification of similar patterns and perceptions of financial vulnerability across different national contexts point to the role of contextual economic, institutional, organisational circumstances and previous level of financial vulnerability in affecting the dynamics of financial vulnerability and the effectiveness of resilience measures. This highlights advantages and limitations of a universalistic approach in the analysis of responses to global crises.

The pandemic has exacerbated the risks associated with financial vulnerability and it is likely to steepen the slowdown in potential growth over the next decade. Investigating its impact at local level and what immediate measures are vital to support the recovery and foster resilience locally is important to inform responses that will shape our future for years to come.

2 Financial Vulnerability

*Emanuele Padovani, Silvia Iacuzzi,
Susana Jorge, and Liliana Pimentel*

Introduction

Starting from a review of the relevant theoretical concepts, this chapter proposes a framework to appreciate how financially vulnerable local governments (LGs) are before and in the immediate aftermath of a global pandemic crisis.

According to McManus et al. (2007, p. 12) vulnerabilities are "components (or links between components) that are likely to have a significant negative impact on an organization." Arunachalam et al. (2017, p. 52) define vulnerable as a local council that, without some structural reform and major revenue and expense adjustments, "is highly unlikely to be able to manage unforeseen financial shocks and any adverse changes in its business and in general economic conditions." In their recent definition, Barbera et al. (2020, p. 533) claim that vulnerability is the "reduced capacity to cope with emerging shocks." There is overall agreement that financial vulnerability is a dimension of financial resilience, which is the capacity to deal with shocks affecting government finances to retain essentially the same functions, structure, and identity (Walker et al., 2002). Yet, financial vulnerability has gone through different conceptualisations and operationalisations.

This chapter considers the different understandings and perspectives of LG financial vulnerability and develops a framework to analyse its multifaceted sources in the immediate aftermath of a pandemic comparing it to the pre-pandemic situation.

Literature overview

A search for LG financial vulnerability in major databases such as Scopus and Web of Science returned only a dozen useful records. The financial vulnerability of public administration has been studied by

DOI: 10.4324/9781003274278-2

scholars at a macroeconomic level for a long time, especially with reference to natural disasters and with a single country perspective (e.g. Pollner et al., 2001). Cepiku and Giordano (2021) provide multifaceted perspectives of the reactions to economic crises by public administrations, highlighting financial vulnerability as one of the factors that shape the choices available to decision makers. At the LG level, the literature on financial vulnerability seems quite scant and mostly related to the global financial crisis of 2008 with different conceptualisations and operationalisations.

The concept of LG financial vulnerability was first used by the Canadian Institute of Chartered Accountants in 2009 (Cabaleiro et al., 2013) as one of the three components, together with flexibility and sustainability, of local financial condition, defined as the ability to meet existing financial obligations, including both public service commitments to residents and businesses and financial commitments to creditors and employees. In this context, the financial vulnerability was understood as "the extent to which the organization depends on resources that are beyond its own control or influence" (Cabaleiro et al., 2013, p. 733).

Indeed, one of the key dimensions of financial vulnerability is precisely the source of local revenues. LGs may both benefit from transfer payments from higher tiers of governments and levy their own taxes and service charges (UCLG, 2019). Despite any guarantee of financial support from central governments in the event of financial rupture, evidence suggests that LGs face more financial risks when they rely on intergovernmental revenues: They are more likely to mismanage public finances due to "moral hazard" (Persson and Tabellini, 1996) and their revenue inflows are more vulnerable, since decisions about them are made by other entities (Martell, 2008; Bastida et al., 2014).

Revenue sources represent just a part of the broader institutional design of power devolution across tiers of government. Comparative LG studies suggest that not only administrative traditions (Pollit and Bouckaert, 2017) but also functional, territorial, and political profiles vary considerably across countries (Kuhlmann and Wollmann, 2014). Looking at functional issues, higher levels of government monitor local budgets and keep local finances under control by establishing specific fiscal governance regimes that may create budget constraints and foster fiscal adaptation and consolidation pressures. Fiscal rules such as limits to current and capital expenditure financing, debt ceilings, balanced budget requirements (e.g. the "golden rule") may impact financial vulnerability (Barbera et al., 2017). Comparative analyses have shown a significant dynamism, differentiation, and complexity of structures and fiscal rules across countries after the 2008 global financial crisis (Geissler et al., 2019). Since institutional factors influence how systems of government respond to crisis (Lodge and Hood, 2012), the structure and type of local revenues, the degree of decentralisation with the scope of local responsibilities and the functions delivered at local level, the supervision and regulation by higher levels of government are all relevant in determining how financially vulnerable LGs are facing the impacts of a global crisis such as the COVID-19 pandemic (OECD, 2020a).

Barbera et al. (2017, p. 675) develop Cabaleiro's concept by maintaining that financial vulnerability is the "result of both external (e.g., dependence on grants) as well as internal (e.g., debt financing, reserves) sources, turning out to be at the interface between the environment and the organization." This perspective emphasises objective sources of financial vulnerability, which include typical elements of financial condition at local level such as the level of diversification of revenues (Mikesell, 2013), the capacity to sell capital assets (Berne and Schramm, 1986), the availability of cash and financial reserves (Downing, 1991; Jacob and Hendrick, 2012), the level of expenditure rigidity, the connected idea of cost stickiness (Cohen et al., 2017) and non-discretionary expenditures (Maher et al., 2020), the capacity to incur short-term liabilities (Berne and Schramm, 1986), the debt burden (Capeci, 1994) or any moratorium on debt repayment (Barbera et al., 2017), and changes in the cash flow on debt covenants (Ahrens and Ferry, 2020). Cepiku et al. (2016) affirm that rigid and sticky expenditures, such as expenses that cannot be deferred such as personnel and debt servicing, may also make it challenging to redirect expenditures to support local communities when unemployment and social inequality increase and the demand for social services rises. The literature also suggests other factors local or central governments may decide upon and which could limit financial vulnerability when facing a crisis: Ahrens and Ferry (2020) mention insurance for low-probability high-impact event; Barbera et al. (2017) provide evidence about an anticipated approval for supplementary budgets, while Hochrainer (2006) talks generally about provisions for contingent credit.

Therefore, when looking at financial vulnerability, it is important to consider both its external and internal dimensions: on the one hand, the administrative structure and fiscal rules LGs are subject to should be considered, and on the other hand, the local financial condition with specific issues related to local revenues and expenditures should not be neglected because the efficacy of the anti-COVID measures depends on the actual situation in each local community.

Furthermore, when analysing resilience with respect to the financial crisis and consequent austerity measures stemming from the credit crunch in 2008, Barbera et al. (2017, p. 675) maintain that "rather than an objective measure of vulnerability, it is the perceived vulnerability which proved to be central in understanding patterns of financial resilience." Indeed, LG, on the one hand, often lacks situation and perspective awareness, sense-making, and systems to control and manage risks, and on the other, they do not often enjoy transforming capacities to implement radical changes or even adapting capacities to implement incremental changes. By relying too much on buffering capacities, organisations tend to "bounce back" or maintain a status quo, rather than develop the capacities needed to change and progress (Barbera et al., 2017, 2019): Rather than leading the change to the next normal, LGs often find themselves chasing after it. Hence, Steccolini et al. (2017, p. 232) conclude that financial vulnerability represents the "perceived exposure to shocks, that is the level and sources of vulnerability and their development over time." Anessi-Pessina et al. further clarify that "vulnerability is the level of perceived exposure to a specific shock and lies at the interface between shocks and organizational capacities" (2020, p. 960). In other words, it is the sense of being able to control financial vulnerability or influence its sources that affect the way in which shocks are interpreted and subsequently tackled, so much that perceived vulnerabilities play a central role in the anticipatory capacity to face shocks which is, in turn, essential for the implementation of bouncing forward capacities (Barbera et al., 2019). Yet, available information has proved to be highly insufficient to help appreciate the level of financial vulnerability, let alone putting in place effective coping capacities during the COVID-19 crisis (Ahrens and Ferry, 2020).

All in all, considering the discussions in the above literature, three relevant dimensions of financial vulnerability can, thus, be singled out:

a Financial vulnerability related to the external institutional design of local administrative structure and fiscal rules; this dimension considers each local authority as an entity embedded in its environment, considering the contingencies created by administrative tradition, rules, and decisions set by higher levels of government;

b Financial vulnerability related to internal issues of financial condition, described by such generally accepted financial indices as financial dependency ratios, debt burden, and revenue-expenses balance; this dimension considers each local authority as a single business entity;

c Financial vulnerability related to the perception of the capacity to cope with a crisis; this is a more context-related dimension that also considers the availability of information and its interpretation.

A conceptual framework

This framework considers internal, external, and perceived dimensions of financial vulnerability, deriving different perspectives for analysis. In turn, each dimension of financial vulnerability can affect different fields investigated to appreciate it. As seen in the literature overview, the external dimension is characterised by outside forces and institutional factors (Lodge and Hood, 2012; Kuhlmann and Wollmann, 2014; Pollitt and Bouckaert, 2017). These, in turn, concern different administrative structures, for example the level of centralisation vis à vis the level of autonomy of LGs, as well as different fiscal rules, i.e. centrally defined policies including the structure, basis, and controllability of major revenue sources, debt rules, investment guidelines, monitoring systems, tax limits, etc., which shape local room for manoeuver during a crisis (Steccolini et al., 2017).

Moreover, local revenue and expenditure structure are influenced both by external institutional factors as well as by internal financial condition. For example, in the aftermath of the 2008 financial crisis, austerity measures at higher levels filtered down to the local level and impacted the resources available to deliver services to local communities (Brusca et al., 2015). On the contrary, with the COVID-19 pandemic, many higher government tiers supported local authorities less able to collect local taxes and tariffs (OECD, 2020a). Indeed, in the face of lockdowns and economic standstills, revenues become ever more uncertain because tax bases shrink, while unemployment and social inequality increase, thereby increasing the demand for social services (Pollitt and Bouckaert, 2017). At the same time, their rigidity may make increasing expenditures to support local communities impossible. Moreover, high levels of debt may lead to non-controllable liabilities and financial risks or there may be rules regarding debt ceilings preventing to resort to debt for extra resources. Moreover, the OECD and the World Bank observed that central government support to local authorities during crises is often ad hoc and unplanned and can create large implicit contingent liabilities (OECD and World Bank, 2019).

Lastly, the perception of the capacity to cope with a crisis is characterised not only by administrative structures, fiscal rules, and revenue and expenditure structure but also by the outlook regarding LGs' ability to manage their internal capacities and to use and shape the external environment to weather a crisis (Steccolini et al., 2017).

Therefore, four fields of enquiry can be singled out in investigating the three dimensions of financial vulnerability before and in the aftermath of a pandemic crisis: (1) the overall administrative structure and fiscal rules, (2) the local revenue structure, (3) the local expenditure structure, and (4) the vulnerability outlook or forecast. Table 2.1 summarises the four fields of enquiry that are relevant to assess the level of financial vulnerability. It does so by providing the main questions that should be answered in order to grasp the essential aspects in two points in time: before the pandemic and in its immediate aftermath. The answers to these questions allow them to understand the impact of the pandemic on financial vulnerability.

Applying the framework

The following chapters use such conceptual framework to appreciate the impact of the COVID-19 pandemic on local finances in eight countries, thus providing a comparative case study analysis. Evidence has been collected through secondary empirical sources such as laws, regulations, and institutional official reports, as well as conversations and workshops with top public officials and direct involvement in data collection and analysis of the impact of COVID-19 on local finances, while the pandemic exerted its effects in its immediate aftermath. The interpretation of the data collected in the specific context is guaranteed by the country experts who have been involved in each country chapter. Not only this guarantees a correct cultural and language appreciation (in this study, we cover contexts with six different languages) but allows us to have an informed, first-hand, and plausible interpretation of the consequences of the impacts of COVID-19 in each different context.

This exercise allows, on the one hand, to better understand financial vulnerability in practice and, on the other hand, to investigate whether, where, and how it changed over time with the pandemic offering both a time and a geographical perspective, because the framework helps investigate LG financial vulnerability across different countries before and in the immediate aftermath of the pandemic. Hence, it can help reveal whether the impact of the pandemic and the efficacy of the measures to contrast COVID-related financial impacts depend on internal or external contingencies and the interplay across the different fields and dimensions.

Table 2.1 A conceptual framework to appreciate local government (LG) financial vulnerability

Before COVID-19	In the immediate aftermath	Vulnerability dimensions
1. Administrative structure and fiscal rules What are the functions of LGs? What is the set of administrative and fiscal rules that apply? What are the institutional relationships between LGs and central governments (and/or regional/state government) in terms of intergovernmental transfers, level of dependency, bailout capacity? What is the role of the administrative structure and the fiscal rules on LG financial vulnerability?	**1. Administrative structure and fiscal rules** What are the first decisions that have been taken by the central (and regional) governments to face local financial distress that affected the administrative structure and fiscal rules, if any?	(a)
2. Revenue structure What are the types of revenues local authorities rely on, with particular emphasis on the basis (is it affected by COVID-19) and rate (who decides)? Are there relevant differences across entities, i.e. different revenues structures for different LGs? (e.g. LGs that rely more on transfers than own revenues, LGs that rely more on business tax than service fees, etc.)	**2. Revenue structure** What are the first decisions that have been taken by the central (regional) government to face COVID-19 related to revenues (e.g. procrastination of revenue collection, cancellation of taxes for certain types of businesses, relief grants)?	(a) and (b)
3. Expenditure structure How rigid are local expenditures? What are the services provided by the LG? Are there relevant differences across entities, i.e. different expenditures for different LGs? (e.g. LGs that run hospitals, care homes, tourist sites, cultural services, etc.)	**3. Expenditure structure** What were the direct consequences of COVID-19 (e.g. more sanitisation expenditures, higher police control, closure of schools with reduction of costs, etc.)? What are the first decisions that have been taken by the central (regional) government to face COVID-19 related to expenditures (e.g. postponement of debt instalments, deferral of transfers to other governments, …)?	(a) and (b)

(Continued)

Table 2.1 A conceptual framework to appreciate local government (LG) financial vulnerability (*Continued*)

Before COVID-19	In the immediate aftermath	Vulnerability dimensions
4. Forecasts How forecasts were approached by central (and regional) government and by LGs, usually (e.g. historic perspective, analysis of economic cycles in the medium-short run, etc.)? How LG financial vulnerability was measured?	**4. Forecasts** What are the expected impacts on local finances? In the short run? In the medium run? How many LGs will face financial distress? Had LGs room for manoeuvres (financial buffers, rainy days funds, …) to (partially) face the crisis? Has the central government or the association of LGs provided a sensitivity analysis/stress test to forecast the impacts? If so, was the analysis carried out by surveying local authorities about their perceived effects on their budget? Or how? How financial LG vulnerability is measured?	(b) and (c)

However, in this context, it should not be forgotten that the framework covers the time up to the so-called "first wave" of the pandemic that is the spring and summer of 2020. Thus, it considers only the short-term effects of the measures taken to counter the impact of the pandemic on local financial vulnerability. This alerts to the temporal dimension that Pollitt (2008) considers crucial in many public policies and management problems, which is that there might be a time-lag effect, so that despite the approval of new regulations that shape the external institutional design or the internal conditions for revenues and expenditures, their consequences might become evident only at a later stage. Moreover, some measures to counteract financial vulnerability in the short run might have the opposite effect on resilience in the long run. For example, Barbera et al. (2019) point out that increasing taxes and fees, deferring investments, reducing the costs, the scope or the size of services or of the organisation, as well as selling assets may all be components of bouncing back strategies, such as retrenchment, buffering, downsizing, cutbacks. Yet, in the long run, such strategies may not favour resilience as they would imply cutting back public functions, while bouncing forward strategies such as transformation, repositioning, and reorientation would support it. Hence, in a time dynamic perspective, bouncing back strategies may help reduce financial vulnerability in the aftermath of a crisis, but not necessarily help resilience in the long run.

Therefore, it is important to keep in mind the benefits as well as the drawbacks of a tool developed in the midst of a crisis, which can reveal helpful at similar time and in similar situations, but might not be applicable or result distortive and misguiding if applied in different conditions.

Moreover, the analysis is limited to the financial aspects of vulnerability and does not take into consideration non-financial elements. As discussed by previous studies, leadership (Cepiku and Giordano, 2021) as well as managerial tools and capacities (Barbera et al., 2019) shape the capacity of reacting to crises and are, therefore, intertwined with financial vulnerability. As a matter of fact, the ways elected and public officials interpret, measure, communicate, and take actions to face crises have an important role not only in shaping financial vulnerability – as considered in point (c) of our framework – but also, in turn, impact other dimensions of vulnerability (e.g. managerial capacity, political issues, policymaking, etc.). Also, the inherent financial elements of vulnerability – normally included in points (a) and (b) of our framework – affect themselves the non-financial aspects of LG vulnerability. This represents a possible frontier for further research in this field which goes beyond the remits of this volume.

3   Australia

Andrea Wallace and Brian Dollery

Country profile: Australia

Population	25.7 million inhabitants (2020)
Government system	Federal parliamentary and constitutional monarchy
Territorial organisation	States and federal territories, and local governments or municipalities or councils
Number of LGs	537 councils (55% are regional, rural or remote councils) (2020)
LG average size	47,237 inhabitants; 59% of municipalities have fewer than 20,000 inhabitants

Sources: OECD/UCLG (2019); Australian Bureau of Statistics https://www.abs.gov.au/; Australian Local Government Association https://alga.asn.au/facts-and-figures/.

Introduction

In contrast to many other advanced countries, including Britain, Canada, Japan, and the United States (Stewart and Smith, 2007), but in common with New Zealand, Australian state, and territory local government (LG) systems provide a relatively limited range of functions, concentrated mainly on "services to property." Unlike many other LG systems, they all provide comparatively few "services to people," such as education and police, which in Australia are the primary responsibility of state governments rather than LGs. Councils typically fall under the control of (part-time) councillors and an indirectly elected mayor, both of whom face periodic elections and oversee the operations of professional staff led by a general manager.

The chief responsibilities of Australian councils in all state and territory LG systems centre on the provision of local infrastructure, like local roads, parks and recreation facilities, public swimming pools and sewage systems, and local services, such as building inspection services, domestic waste management, health inspection services, and street cleaning. However, over the past few decades, the range of local

DOI: 10.4324/9781003274278-3

services provided by Australian LG systems has increased (Dollery et al., 2006). Service provision now often embraces some community facilities, like aged care facilities and childcare facilities, as well as some strategic roles, including local economic development, tourism, and urban renewal. In addition, some services traditionally delivered by federal and state governments have been devolved to local author-ities, such as some community health services, pollution regulation, and regional airports.

This chapter focuses on nine New South Wales (NSW) local authorities in three separate categories, namely metropolitan coun-cils, regional towns/cities, and large rural councils. This group serves as a sample of Australian councils with population per cat-egories of 73 to 243 thousand, 44 to 75 thousand, and 6 to 13 thou-sand residents, respectively. The limitation of the analysis is to not to include the impact of the pandemic on larger Australian cites such as Brisbane (Queensland), with a population of 1.3 million, and other larger councils. However, these amount to 3% of the total number of Australian LGs.

Ku-ring-gai Council, City of Parramatta, and Waverley Council are metropolitan councils characterised by a dense population, on average 4,000 residents per square km, with a comparatively low infrastruc-ture backlog ratio and with less than 10% of the population receiving pensioner rate concessions (OLG, 2018). Typically, these councils possess a larger rating base to fund their operations. Due to their urban nature, most metropolitan councils are not subject to external shocks like extreme weather events and bushfires. Regional towns/ cities, represented by Coffs Harbour City, Lismore City, and Tamworth City Councils in the present context, and large rural councils, such as Blayney Shire, Gunnedah Shire, and Uralla Shire councils, are different in several respects; they are spatially dispersed over large areas, have a smaller, older population, and a lower property tax base from which to fund council costs. For exam-ple, population density in these regional towns/cities is, on average, 35 residents per square km, while it can be as low as 1.9 residents per square km in large rural councils like the Uralla Shire. Large rural councils – and regional towns to some extent – face an ongoing financial stress due to population loss. Over recent years, bushfires and severe drought has spawned intensifying financial problems. In 2020, the potential for substantive economic regeneration of many of the drought-affected LG areas has been limited by the onset of the COVID-19 pandemic.

Administrative structure and fiscal rules

Understanding vulnerability before COVID-19

Australia is a federation with three tiers of government: Commonwealth or national government, eight state and territory governments, and a LG system in all states and territories, except the Australian Capital Territory. However, LG in Australia does not enjoy constitutional recognition and it is thus a "creature of statute" in the legal systems of the respective state or territory governments. Accordingly, LG is often referred to as the "poor cousin" of national and state governments in the Australian political milieu.

A striking feature of Australian fiscal federalism resides in its high degree of vertical fiscal imbalance. This arises from the fact that the Commonwealth government enjoys much greater powers of taxation than its state and territory counterparts (Dollery, 2002). In particular, unlike state and territory governments, the Commonwealth imposes income taxes, as well as a Goods and Service Tax (GST). By contrast, the Commonwealth has comparatively limited expenditure responsibilities, with state and territory governments providing both public health and public education.

In order to address the imbalance between the revenue-raising and expenditure responsibilities of the different tiers of government, over the past century, the Australian federation developed a sophisticated and depoliticised system of intergovernmental transfers through the Commonwealth Grants Commission (Morris, 2002). These transfers include funds to LG paid through Financial Assistance Grants (FAGs) by the Commonwealth Grants Commission.

In addition, state and territory governments also engage in intergovernmental transfers to the local councils in their respective LG systems through state LG Grants Commissions. These transfers have two main components: a General Purpose Component (GPC) and the Local Roads Component (LRC). GPC funds can be employed to finance most municipal activities whereas LRC funds are intended for local road systems.

Australian LG is characterised by immense diversity. For example, population size varies from just 742 residents in Wiluna Shire Council in Western Australia (ABS, 2020) to 1,131,155 people in Brisbane City Council in 2016 (ABS, 2020a). Similarly, population density differs greatly, as evidenced by Burnside in South Australia with 1,630 residents per square km and Flinders Council in Tasmania with 0.45 residents per square km. In recent years, larger cities have attempted to play a more substantial role in fostering economic development, as well as climate change adaptation (Betsill and Bulkeley, 2006).

The immense variation between LG entities in all Australian LG systems makes it not only difficult, but also unwise to try to draw generalised conclusions regarding the capacity and performance of LG authorities. For example, while frequently large councils possess superior policy capacity compared with their smaller cousins, this is by no means always the case, especially when groups of small councils collaborate in terms of policymaking capacity through regional alliances and the like. Similarly, whereas urban councils often find it easier to recruit high-level policy skills, compared with their regional, rural, and remote counterparts, numerous non-metropolitan local authorities nonetheless enjoy excellent policy capacity.

Australia is a large federated country comprised of different states and territories, each with its own characteristics. It is accordingly difficult to generalise about LG administrative structures and fiscal rules. In order to understand the vast differences between LGs across the nation, Australian municipalities are grouped into different classifications in a taxonomic system known as the Australian Classification of LG (ACLG), which is determined by the Australian Bureau of Statistics (ABS). Further groupings are applied by the NSW Office of LG (OLG) to better reflect the heterogeneous nature of the NSW LG. NSW councils are grouped into five categories that are based on broad demographic variables, such as population, population density, and population growth (OLG, 2019).

Immediate reaction to COVID-19

The administrative structure and fiscal rules operating within Australian fiscal federalism have remained unchanged in the immediate aftermath of the COVID-19 pandemic. Thus, the taxation structure remains the same and ongoing intergovernmental transfers have not been affected. Moreover, given the comparative success of the Australian approach to the COVID-19 pandemic, together with an ongoing vaccination program, there is little prospect that Australian fiscal federalism will experience any permanent changes.

Revenue structure

Understanding vulnerability before COVID-19

Australian LG is funded through a combination of property taxes (known colloquially as "rates"), fees, and charges for services, intergovernmental grants, developer charges, and other miscellaneous sources (Dollery et al., 2006). On average, local authorities raise around 91% of their own revenue, with property tax income constituting 36% of aggregate local revenue, and grants and subsidies comprising about 9% (Australian Government, 2010, p. 12). In international terms, this represents a relatively high degree of financial self-sufficiency. However, these averages mask a striking degree of variation between councils, with marked differences between metropolitan, regional, and rural councils, as a result of substantial variations in population size, tax bases, and the capacity to impose user charges. For example, the percentage of revenue as operational grants varies between 5% and 6% in metropolitan councils, between 6% and 15% in rural towns/cities, and between 15% and 35% in large rural councils. Similarly, the percentage of revenues as capital grants are lower in metropolitan councils, varying between 7% and 17%, while in a regional town such as Tamworth, capital grants represent 20% of revenue. In the Blayney Shire council, a large rural council, capital grants represent 35% of revenue (OLG, 2018).

There are marked differences between metropolitan, regional, and rural council sources of revenue. In terms of both the Commonwealth Grants Commission formula Australian government and the NSW state government intergovernmental grant procedures, which employ "disability factors" to calculate the quantum of grants, rural councils are treated advantageously. Moreover, the demographic profile of the three categories of councils typically differs considerably, with regional towns/cities and large rural councils containing a greater percentage of older residents, lower income residents, and Aboriginal and Torres Straits Island (ATSIC) residents. Additionally, both absolute population levels and population densities are lower in rural and regional LG areas. This limits the ability of regional and rural councils to reap economies of scale in service provision, as well as economies of density. The demographic characteristics of regional and rural local authorities constrain their capacity to increase property taxes as well as municipal fees and charges.

Immediate reaction to COVID-19

The most important revenue policy change in 2020 has little to do with the pandemic. The NSW Government had requested its agency the Independent Pricing and Regulatory Tribunal to assess the property tax regime in NSW LGs. In response to the subsequent IPART report *Review of the Local Government Rating System 2016* – released in 2019 – the NSW Government published its Local Government Amendment

Bill 2021. This legislation sought to introduce various changes to the LG rating system in response to the IPART report. This included changes to the regulations regarding post-merger property taxes in amalgamated councils. Following the 2016 NSW municipal merger program, 17 new forcibly consolidated councils were created and they were required to "harmonise" property taxes across their new LG areas to equalise the tax burden on all local residents. These 17 councils faced difficult financial problems that were aggravated by the pandemic. The Local Government Amendment Bill 2021 *inter alia* enables these merged municipalities to gradually harmonise rates over up to four years to help protect property owners from excessive and sudden property tax rises. In addition, the Local Government Amendment Bill 2021 permits councils to create more flexible residential, business, and farmland property tax subcategories. This enables them to set fairer property taxes to more accurately reflect access to local services and local infrastructure.

Expenditure structure

Understanding vulnerability before COVID-19

In NSW, metropolitan, regional, and rural councils all have differing expenditure profiles due in part to their different fiscal capacities. Major expenditures for the 2018/19 financial year for each of the nine representative NSW councils include employee costs and materials and contracts. The former averages 31% of total expenditure in regional town/cities, reaching about 42% on average in metropolitan or large rural councils. Materials and contracts form a significant part of expenditure, about one third, in regional town/cities councils (OLG, 2018).

Immediate reaction to COVID-19

In the immediate wake of COVID-19, municipal expenditure was dramatically altered by the stimulus packages introduced by both the NSW Government and the councils themselves in order to maintain economic activity at the local level. Table 3.1 summarises the COVID stimulus packages offered by the nine NSW councils.

As shown in Table 3.1, the nine sample local councils played a significant role in their local communities via economic stimulus packages. These included "Buy Local" strategies for procurement, accelerating invoice payment to local suppliers, and rent support for businesses and individuals renting council-owned property. In addition, many councils

Table 3.1 COVID-19 economic stimulus packages by council

Council	Council initiated stimulus
Blayney Shire Council	• Social Media Photograph Competition, two prizes of an AU$50 takeaway voucher each week. • Council committed to a Buy Local/Local Procurement Policy.
Coffs Harbour City Council	• "Buy local" campaign. • Local procurement policy for council. • Remove account, reminder, and credit card fees and surcharges. • Loan repayment relief for existing loans to community groups. • Rent relief, or rent waivers for businesses and community groups renting council-owned buildings from 1 April 2020 to 30 June 2020. • Coffs Harbour Grants finder open to all individuals, businesses, and community groups.
Gunnedah Shire Council	• Grant writers made available to local businesses. • Council committed to retaining staff without Federal Assistance. • "Buy local" campaign. • Council Local procurement policy amended; for example, 80% of Salesyard Master plan delivery will use AU$14.2M of local suppliers and contactors. • Refunds for undetermined development applications. • AU$1.6M COVID-19 Business Support Package. • AU$28M Capital Works Program Escalated.
Ku-ring-gai Council	• AU$100,000 in community grants. • Hiring fees for council-owned venues suspended or refunded.
Lismore City Council	• Community groups renting council-owned properties will have rent waived. • "Buy local" campaign.
City of Parramatta	• Local procurement policy for council. • Faster payment by council to local suppliers (within 7 days of invoicing). • On-street parking regulations relaxed. • Local food business directory promoted by council. • Small business grants of up to AU$2,000 (total pool AU$100,000).

(*Continued*)

Table 3.1 COVID-19 economic stimulus packages by council (*Continued*)

Council	Council initiated stimulus
Tamworth Regional Council	• Tamworth Regional Trading Directory. • Click and collect library services. • Virtual programs in lieu of usual programs, e.g. story time for children. • Free access to Grants Hub. • Fast tracking invoice payments. • Working with small businesses to ensure the small business receives all economic assistance it's entitled to. • Support for community organisations leasing council properties.
Waverley Council	• Buy local campaign. • Local Procurement policy for council. • Pay local suppliers within 15 days of invoicing. • Rent support for businesses operating from council owned premises. • Current capital works program, valued at AU$50 M.
Uralla Shire Council	• No stimulus packages or information offered.

Sources: BSC (2020); CoP (2020); CHCC (2020); GSC (2020); KRGC (2020); LCC (2020); The Armidale Express (2020); TRC (2020); WC (2020).

collected local business information for their residents to provide local communities with a reliable source of information about local business services. Other forms of assistance were also offered. For example, both the Tamworth Regional Council and the Gunnedah Shire Council hired professional grant writers to assist local businesses seek "other-source" funding. In LG areas, where small business played a dominant role in the local economy, such as Waverley, Parramatta, and Ku-ring-gai, council administered own-source grants were provided to local businesses.

In the immediate aftermath of COVID-19, municipal expenditure was also affected through economic stimulus packages offered by the NSW Government. These economic stimulus package from the NSW government to the nine NSW sample councils included regulatory fees and administration costs waived until June 2020 in all councils, except the Blayney Shire and Uralla Shire councils (BSC, 2020; CoP, 2020; CHCC, 2020; GSC, 2020; KRGC, 2020; LCC, 2020; The Armidale Express, 2020; TRC, 2020; WC, 2020). The NSW Government financially supported councils to pass-on some benefits to businesses and individuals in their local areas, such as delayed fees and the relaxation of municipal business regulations. This support ranged from waiving the cost of business licence renewals, increasing outdoor dining areas, waiving fees, as well as postponing rent and property tax payments. However, as demonstrated in Table 3.1, not all councils were able to pass-on NSW Government stimulus to their communities. For example, the rural Uralla and Blayney councils did not inform residents of the stimulus package from the NSW Government, perhaps because they were not financially able to implement these measures.

A striking feature of the COVID stimulus provided by the NSW Government was the rapidity of its delivery. Table 3.2 summarises the timely nature of the COVID stimulus.

Table 3.2 Timeline of NSW government economic stimulus to local government

Date	Stimulus action
8 April 2020	Splinter award negotiated for NSW council employees. The employment award designed to protect employees whose positions have affected by COVID-19.
9 April 2020	AU$82M committed to support 260 local government childcare centres ineligible for Jobkeeper payments.
16 April 2020	Regional Infrastructure projects fast tracked, with AU$25M made available for councils to upgrade 171 showgrounds in NSW, and a new COVID-19 recovery ward constructed at Royal North Shore Hospital.
17 April 2020	Regulatory changes enacted so that NSW councils can defer 2020/21 rates notices for one month.
	Councils can also waive or reduce fees for local COVID-19 affected businesses, such as food premises or hairdressers.
	Council documents are not required to be available for inspection at council chambers if available electronically.
26 April 2020	AU$395M Local Government Economic Stimulus package announced.
	The package is comprised of:
	AU$112.5M to safeguard council jobs (excludes casual and fixed term staff, as well as senior staff).
	AU$250M increase in low-cost loans from TCorp.
	AU$32.8M Emergency Services Levy increased will be covered by NSW Government.
4 May 2020	AU$500,000 funding boost for NSW council-run animal shelters. The funding will cover vet expenses, food, and minor maintenance.
5 May 2020	AU$10M in enhanced e-planning to ensure planned construction and projects are continued.

Sources: LGNSW (2020); NSW Government 2020 (2020a, 2020b, 2020c); Roberts (2020).

The Australian Government responded quickly to provide additional economic stimulus packages to LG. In early March 2020, all 537 Australian local councils were contacted by the Commonwealth Government and asked to identify a suitable land, transport, or infrastructure project that could be started within a six-month time period and that was eligible for funding under the Commonwealth Infrastructure Investment Program (ALGA, 2020). By May 2020, Australian Government announced its AU$500 million Roads and Infrastructure stimulus package for "shovel ready" projects.

Each of the nine councils was allocated a portion of the AU$500 million Commonwealth Government's Roads and Infrastructure stimulus package. In the particular case of the nine councils analysed here, metropolitan councils received, on average, AU$756,000, slightly more than large rural councils, who received on average AU$715,000. These regional towns/cities, on the other hand, received substantially larger roads and Infrastructure stimulus program, on average AU$1.7 million (ALGA, 2020). The funding allocation was based upon road length, the population of each LG area, as well as further recommendations from the Commonwealth Local Government Grants Commission (Skatssoon, 2020).

Vulnerability outlook

Understanding vulnerability before COVID-19

All Australian LG systems have been subjected to periodic inquiries into their financial sustainability, including NSW LG. As part of its *Fit for the Future* LG reform program, the NSW Government had established the Independent Local Government Review Panel in 2011 to inquire into the ongoing financial sustainability of NSW LG. In its final report *Revitalizing Local Government,* the panel argued that there were too many councils in NSW and that many councils were not fiscally viable in the long run. It, thus, recommended a radical council consolidation process that was implemented by the NSW Government.

Immediate reaction to COVID-19

At present, no systematic inquiry has examined the financial vulnerability of NSW in the aftermath of the COVID pandemic. However, it is likely that some councils, especially merged municipalities, face difficult financial challenges in the future.

Final remarks

In common with LG systems worldwide, Australian LG has been adversely affected by the COVID pandemic. Timely intervention by the national government, as well as state and territory governments, offered financial assistance to local councils, as well as various categories of local residents. This has undoubtedly assisted in stabilising LG, including NSW LG. While it is still too early to assess the long-run impact of the COVID pandemic, it would appear that little will change in the future. The comparative success of the Commonwealth and state governments in tackling the pandemic and limiting its adverse economic and health impacts seems to have largely protected Australian LG.

4 Austria

Thomas Prorok and Robert Blöschl

Country profile: Austria

Population	8.9 million inhabitants (2019)
Government system	Unitary state and parliamentary democracy
Territorial organisation	Three tiers, federal state, states (*Länder*), and municipalities (*Gemeinden*)
Number of LGs	2,096 municipalities (2019)
LG average size	4,227 inhabitants; 55% of municipalities have fewer than 2,000 inhabitants

Sources: OECD/UCLG (2019); Statistik Austria https://www.statistik.at/web_de/ statistiken/menschen_und_gesellschaft/bevoelkerung/volkszaehlungen_registerzae-hlungen_abgestimmte_erwerbsstatistik/bevoelkerungsstand/index.html.

Introduction

The Austrian Constitution of 1920 defines Austria as a federal state formed by nine states (*Länder*). Within the state level, municipal governments (*Gemeinden*) are granted the right to self-government as independent administrative bodies in their sphere of competence. In sum, the three relevant levels of government are the federal government, state, and municipal level.[1] In principle, the Austrian Constitution entrenches and protects municipalities not only as local administrative units but also as institutions of self-government. This includes the right to self-governance in all matters within their local boundaries, the fulfilment of tasks of self-governance through democratically elected municipal agents, the right to own assets of all kinds and operate economic enterprises, and the possibility to establish local authority associations. According to Mitterer and Prorok (2020), the degree of self-governance is, however, limited by a variety of measures such as:

- Within the delegated sphere of competence, municipalities are obliged to fulfil tasks for the federal and state level;
- All municipalities are expected to fulfil the same tasks not taking into account the differences in size and capacity among municipalities. This can lead to smaller municipalities being dependent

DOI: 10.4324/9781003274278-4

on external expertise and having difficulties to provide services to the full extent;

- The Austrian Constitution foresees that the state-level regulates local government (LG) through their own laws (*Gemeindeordnungen*), thus leading to varying degrees of self-governance throughout the country.

The own autonomous competences of municipalities on this basis, which exist in addition to the competences delegated from the federal or state level, include, in particular, the following areas: traffic and transport; gas, water, and electricity supply; waste collection; sewage disposal; kindergarten, parts of education; elderly care; cemeteries; and cultural and sport facilities are all within the competences of municipal administration.

Administrative structure and fiscal rules

Understanding vulnerability before COVID-19

All municipalities manage their own budget independently. They must prepare an annual budget at the end of the year, which shows in detail which revenues and expenditures are expected for the next year. The local council has to approve the annual budget. In any case, the provision of basic services has to be guaranteed. Municipal budgets are constrained by the Austrian Stability Pact, setting targets for budget deficits, debt, and expenditure growth, and thus limiting their financial scope. The Austrian Stability Pact is the national implementation of the European growth and stability pact (Pleschberger, 2008). Local budgets are overseen by municipal departments at the Länder level and, depending on the region, fall into the sphere of competence of regional courts of auditors. Additionally, municipalities with more than 10,000 inhabitants can be subject of audits by the federal court of auditors (Rauskala and Saliterer, 2015).

A major share of municipal budgets comes from intergovernmental transfers, which is a complex system of re-distribution of revenues across all levels of government. The complex nature of this system leads to unclear competences split among the federal, the state, and the local level (Mitterer et al., 2016). The main part of intergovernmental transfers is ruled by the system of fiscal equalisation, which is agreed upon in a pact among the federal government, state, and municipalities for a period of four to six years. In this system, the financial flows among the levels of government are settled. This affects among other tasks the rights of taxation, the distribution of revenues from the shared federal taxes, and who bear specific costs (Bröthaler et al., 2017). The system has proven to be a central element for securing the financial autonomy of all government levels, due to the fact that all stakeholders have to agree to the pact. However, LGs have limited tax autonomy and at the same time are responsible for a wide variety of tasks. This leads to missing fiscal equivalence, meaning that the responsibility for expenditures, revenues, and tasks diverges (Bauer et al., 2017). In recent years, a shift in financial responsibility from the federal to the local level can be observed. This shift further limits municipal autonomy, thus making LGs more vulnerable in times of crisis.

Immediate aftermath of COVID-19

The economic crisis following the COVID-19 pandemic has widely impacted municipalities as they are responsible for maintaining key infrastructures like streets, schools, kindergartens, water supply, waste collection, and sewage disposal. The immediate reaction on the federal level was a 1 billion investment program for the municipal level. Municipalities could apply for government aid covering 50% of the costs of investment projects. The federal support was, however, weakened by federal tax reform in 2020, leading to lower tax revenues at the federal level and, thus, a reduction of an estimated 1 billion euro in shared tax transfers on the local level. In conflict with the established principle of cooperative federalism, the reform was issued via an initiative not allowing for assessment at the municipal level. The lack of communication among the administrative tiers during the crisis can not only be observed in legislative matters but also in transparency issues. Municipalities were insufficiently supplied with forecasts of shared tax transfers, hence making it difficult to plan their budgets.

Municipal budgets came under pressure because fiscal rules at the local level are rather tight. Following a recommendation by the European Commission, the EU finance ministers decided to pause the execution of the EU stability and growth pact. As an immediate reaction to the COVID-19 crisis, the fiscal rules under the Austrian stability pact, which specifies targets for budget deficit, the level of debt, expenditure growth, etc., have been suspended. In theory, this means a wider fiscal space for reactions to the crisis at the local level. Municipalities are, however, dependent on the reactions at the *Länder* level as there are state-level rules on debt and expenditures. Under normal circumstances, nearly all states prohibit municipalities to take out loans for current expenditures leaving debt financing only for investments in property. The current crisis led to some states granting municipalities wider access to short-term loans, e.g. in Oberösterreich and in Steiermark.

Revenue structure

Understanding vulnerability before COVID-19

In Austria, there are five main sources of municipal revenue:

* Shared tax transfers (around 40% of total operational income);
* Local and municipal taxes (around 20% of total operational income);
* Fees for municipal services including utilities and other educational and social services (around 20% of total operational income);
* Current transfers (around 10% of total operational income);
* Other fees and income sources (around 10% of total operational income).

A major share of municipal budgets comes from intergovernmental transfers, a complex system of re-distribution of revenues across all levels of government regulated in the Intergovernmental Fiscal Relations Act (*Finanzausgleichsgesetz*, FAG), which is negotiated every four to six years in negotiations among the three levels of administration. This Act defines the amount of shared revenues municipalities are granted. One of the main criteria for distribution is the graded population scheme which reflects changes in population in a nonlinear way. Based on this scheme, urban municipalities with larger populations receive a larger share of the revenues. Shared revenues are mainly comprised of shares out of taxes like the value added tax (VAT), income tax, and corporate tax. In total, around 15% of shared revenues are allocated to municipalities in the context of fiscal equalisation (Bröthaler et al., 2017). Shared taxes amounted to 6.7 billion euros in 2018 for the LGs, excluding the capital city of Vienna (Mitterer et al., 2020).

In comparison to other countries, Austria is a country with high taxation on labour and low taxation on property. This is a weakness in times of crisis as taxes are highly dependent on the economic development and, thus, are subject to fluctuations (OECD, 2020c). For Austrian municipalities, this not only manifests itself in unstable shared taxes but also changing levels of local taxes. Local taxes are an important factor of municipal income. The most important local tax for municipalities' budgets is the municipal tax.[2] Therefore, municipalities with higher employment have higher municipal tax income. In general, this applies stronger to urban LGs and municipalities with strong tourism industry. Property tax is levied on individuals owning property, the amount is set by the municipalities considering a legal tax cap. As there has not been a reform since 1973, the property tax is currently under revision and likely to be reformed in the next years (Geissler and Ebinger, 2019; Mühlberger and Ott, 2016). Municipal tax amounted to about 2.5 billion euros in 2018 whereas property tax amounted to about 600 million euros (all municipalities except Vienna) (Mitterer et al., 2020).

Besides shared revenues, there is a further intergovernmental transfer system between municipalities and the federal and state level. Within this system, the states and also the federal government distribute transfers to support municipal expenditures. These transfers can be divided into current transfers and capital transfers. Current transfers are meant to finance the provision of public services. Capital transfers can support investments in infrastructure. Current transfers amounted to 1.6 billion euro in 2018 with current transfers from the federal level amounting to 20% and from the state level to 60%. Municipalities that are under fiscal distress (e.g. because of losses in municipal tax revenue or structural issues) are granted additional transfers from the state to cover the deficit. However, in such a situation, all further investments are subject to approval by the state, who monitor municipalities until a sustainable and balanced budget is reached. Through this transfer system, rural LGs benefit more as levies are higher for municipalities with more income.

Fees are mainly generated through the provision of public services and utilities such as water, sewerage, and waste. There are, however, local authority associations that carry out these services and have their own budget. In this case, municipalities make proportionate payments to cover the costs of the associations.

To conclude, important expenditure-incurring tasks such as health care and social protection happen at subnational level, but a minor share is financed through municipal revenues. As a result, municipalities are financially dependent mainly on the shared tax transfers by higher levels of government due to the significant mismatch between revenue-raising power and expenditure responsibilities (European Commission, 2019). While the shared tax transfers and local tax incomes are higher in urban LGs, after mandatory transfers (levies, current, and capital transfers) the income of rural LGs becomes more levelled with that of urban ones.

Immediate aftermath of COVID-19

In March 2020, the Austrian government announced a variety of measures in order to contain the spread of the COVID-19 virus. With the exemption of grocery stores, pharmacies and other basic services retail stores were closed. Schools and universities had to shift to home and online schooling and a general lockdown limited social contacts. The measures undertaken led to a massive economic down-turn hitting some sectors especially hard such as accommodation and gastronomy, production and retail (Czypionka et al., 2020).

The economic downturn has impacted municipalities mainly on three levels: the shared tax transfers, the municipal tax, and the tourist tax. According to estimations from December 2020, municipalities would have likely to lose around 1.5 billion euros of income per year in 2020 and 2021. Thus, total losses could have amounted up to 3 billion euros for the two years. Shared tax transfers to municipalities were expected to fall substantially because of reduced income tax and corporate tax revenues on the federal level. Based on federal estimations, shared tax transfers would have decreased around 992 million euros in 2020 and another 282 million euros in 2021. Job losses and short-time work in the private sector led to reduced levels of municipal tax. Municipal tax was expected to make up around 260 to 290 million euros of losses. Tourism tax decrease by 100 to 180 million euros in 2020 was expected. In 2021, a recovery seemed possible, but there was the expectation not to reach the pre-crisis-level (Biwald and Mitterer, 2020).

These losses on the local level were only partly compensated by the federal level, thus leading to substantial budgetary problems. While the first federal aid program concentrated on investments (see below), the second aid program contained 0.4 billion euros in replacements for losses in shared taxes (Badelt, 2021).

Additionally, in some Austrian regions, the Länder level partly compensated income losses, such as losses in Kindergarten fees and losses in municipal taxes.

Expenditure structure

Understanding vulnerability before COVID-19

LGs in Austria perform their own autonomous functions as well as tasks delegated by the federal and state level. Municipalities cover a wide range of tasks from the construction and maintenance of streets to kindergartens, primary schools, residential care homes for elderly people and services like water supply, sewerage, and waste disposal (Geißler and Ebinger, 2019).

Particularly in the last two decades, the municipalities in Austria have increasingly become service providers for citizens rather than being mere administrative authorities. As there is no difference regarding the size or population in the Federal Constitutional Law, fulfilling all these local responsibilities can be challenging especially for small Austrian municipalities. However, the lack of differentiation has disadvantages for larger regional centres too, as their function as a regional service provider is not taken into account.

Highest municipal expenditures are born in the provision of utility services (e.g. water, sewerage, waste), welfare, and education (Mitterer et al., 2020). Expenditure has to follow the approved budget. If deviations from the budget occur (e.g. because of unforeseen projects), municipalities have to prepare a revised budget and gain the approval of the local council.

The main areas of capital spending are street building and service provision for water, sewerage, and waste. They accounted for almost half of all capital spending in 2019. In recent years, investments in full-time schools and kindergartens have increased rapidly (Biwald and Mitterer, 2020). In general, municipalities are only allowed to take on long-term debt for capital spending. Current expenditures cannot be covered with long-term debt. There are rules for short-term loans which have to be paid back within the fiscal year. Furthermore, *Länder* law prohibits the use of risky financial instruments. Over the last ten years, municipal debt slightly rose from 11.5 billion euro in 2009 to 11.6 billion in 2018 (Mitterer et al., 2020).

Immediate aftermath of COVID-19

At the local level, current expenditures could not be reduced. The introduced short-work scheme for the private sector has not been applied to LGs. Personnel costs, therefore, did not significantly change. The same accounts for other administrative costs which could not be reduced to continue providing municipal services. Municipalities even had to face higher costs for sanitation equipment, to provide testing and vaccination. The federal level only party compensated these additional current expenditures.

Each state determines levies that all municipalities must transfer, e.g. in order to finance social welfare and public hospitals run by the state. These transfers to the state level are expected to rise which will bring municipal budgets further under pressure.

However, the federal level issued an investment program worth 1 billion euros to guarantee that necessary investments in infrastructure can be carried out in the years 2020 and 2021. The amount is split among all Austrian municipalities according to the number of inhabitants and a graded populations scheme. Municipalities can apply for direct transfers covering up to 50% of their expenditures for maintenance and investment in infrastructure of certain areas like day-care facilities for children, schools, public transport, municipal streets, and water and wastewater management. Transfers are not supposed to be used for current expenditures (BMF, 2020; Mitterer, 2020).

In contrast to the federal and state level, municipalities are legally constrained to compensate liquidity problems with loans. This makes them less flexible in handling crises. As a response to the COVID-19 crisis, some state laws were relaxed allowing municipalities to take out higher short-term loans during the course of the crisis.

Vulnerability outlook

Understanding vulnerability before COVID-19

Vulnerability measurement in Austria is often carried out by calculating performance indicators. There is a widely used set of financial ratios measuring financial health including the public saving ratio, the ratio of available budget, the duration of indebtedness, the rate of self-financing, and the debt service ratio. So far, measurements were based on cash accounting, but with the shift to accrual accounting in 2020, financial health measurements will include balances as well.

The Austrian Association of Cities and Towns regularly publishes a prognosis of municipal finances for the next four years conducted by the Centre for Public Administration Research (KDZ) (Mitterer et al., 2020). Usually, several scenarios are calculated, thus taking into account multiple trajectories.

Immediate aftermath of COVID-19

The COVID-19 crisis gave rise to several surveys among municipalities on their perceptions on the crisis. A survey among 20 cities was conducted in May 2020 (Mitterer and Hochholdinger, 2020). Results showed a growing worry about the future financial situation: 60% of the cities claimed that a municipal aid program for investments was necessary, while 75% called for specific measures for cities to tackle the crisis as they were heavily affected by tax losses and still had to provide a great number of services. 75% of cities estimated that debt levels would rise. An important factor to ensure financial health is seen in the compensation of shared taxes and municipal taxes financed by the federal and state governments.

The pandemic made it necessary to publish regular outlooks on municipal finances. These outlooks had to be adapted according to developments such as federal aid programs or lockdowns, which have heavily influenced the municipalities' financial situation (Mitterer et al., 2021). Except for regular outlook calculations, the pandemic did not lead to major changes in the measurement of financial vulnerability of LGs so far.

Final remarks

The COVID-19 crisis has put municipal budgets under pressure. Revenue losses have been accompanied by stable or even increasing expenditures. In the short-term, the crisis, therefore, has made it necessary for the federal government to compensate fiscal distress at the local level. In the long run, however, further steps should be undertaken. The current crisis once again sheds light on several areas where reform efforts are necessary. The complex intertwinement of public service provision and financial flows has been criticised for years. For a long time, a more transparent distribution of competences among all levels of government as well as the organisational and financial disentanglement of public service provision has been discussed. Nevertheless, these reforms are only been implemented reluctantly, due to constitutional federal structures (Bauer and Biwald, 2019). The COVID-19 crisis could be regarded as a chance to overcome this situation and make a step towards higher resilience in LGs' budgets.

Notes

1 There are some exceptions, however, such as statutory cities which are assigned further responsibilities as well as the capital city of Vienna, which is a municipality and a Land at the same time.
2 Companies based in Austria have to pay municipal tax amounting to 3% of the total sum of salaries paid within one month.

5 Bosnia and Herzegovina

Jelena Poljašević

Country profile: Bosnia and Herzegovina

Population	3.5 million inhabitants (2013)
Government system	Federal state (Federation of Bosnia and Herzegovina – FB&H) unitary state (Republic of Srpska – RS), and parliamentary democracy
Territorial organisation	Three tiers, state (and one city district), cantons (*kantoni*), and municipalities (*općina, opština*)
Number of LGs	144 municipalities (2021)
LG average size	24,700 inhabitants; 58% of municipalities have fewer than 20,000 inhabitants

Sources: OECD/UCLG (2019); Agency for Statistics of Bosnia and Herzegovina, https://bhas.gov.ba/

Introduction

By its organisation, Bosnia and Herzegovina is a complex federal state with elements of the confederation that is administratively divided into two entities, the Federation of Bosnia and Herzegovina (FB&H) and Republic of Srpska (RS), and the Brčko District. The FB&H is comprised of 10 cantons (*kantoni*) which are further divided into 79 municipalities/cities (*općina, opština*). In the Federation, most powers related to local governments (LGs) are vested with the cantons. The territory of the RS consists of 56 municipalities and 8 cities (*opština*). The City of Brčko is a special administrative unit, i.e. a district with the status of LG.

Out of a total of 144 municipalities, 58% have less than 20,000 inhabitants, 38% municipalities have between 20,000 and 100,000 inhabitants, and only 4% have more than 100,000 inhabitants. The main competence of municipality is environmental protection, housing policy, construction and maintenance of municipal infrastructure, local roads and local public transport, pre-school education, basic education (Šnjegota et al., 2019). LGs are required to assess the quality of services provided by public institutions in the fields of health and social protection, education, culture, and sports. In FB&H, cantons

DOI: 10.4324/9781003274278-5

have exclusive responsibility for establishment and monitoring of police forces, educational policy, cultural policy, the development of policy on the regulation and provision of public services, the regulation of local land use, improvement of local business and charity activities the creation and application of a cantonal tourism policy. Thus, cantons have a main role in regulation; they are limited to FB&H and have a limited budget. Municipalities represent, therefore, the most important level of LGs, both in terms of their role in the provision of public services and budget dimensions.

Administrative structure and fiscal rules

Understanding vulnerability before COVID-19

Fiscal discipline and general fiscal status are prescribed by the laws on the budget system and on borrowing and debt. According to the law on the budget system, planned budget resources and planned budget expenditures must be balanced, that is, it is not permitted to propose a budget containing a planned uncovered budget deficit or a planned unallocated budget surplus. The level of indebtedness is prescribed for LGs in a way that LGs can only be indebted in the long term if, during the debt period, the total repayment of proposed and outstanding debt in any subsequent year does not exceed 18% of its operating revenues generated in the previous fiscal year. Short-term debt cannot be higher than 5% of operating revenues generated in the previous fiscal year. The total exposure of the LGs under the guarantees issued may not exceed 30% of the amount of operating revenues generated in the previous fiscal year. An LG is obliged to obtain the approval of the Ministry of Finance (MoF, *Ministarstvo finansija i trezora Bosne i Hercegovine*) for its indebtedness and for the issuance of a debt guarantee, and this consent is valid for one year from the date of issue. LG debt can arise through a credit agreement and the issuance of securities. The law also sets out the conditions under which LGs can borrow; in the short term, for the temporary financing of cash flow deficits and the financing of liabilities from the previous year; and, in the long term, to finance capital investments, refinance existing debt, and finance liabilities arising from the restructuring of LG's subsidiaries. The repayment of an LG debt can be secured by specific revenues from capital investments financed by debt and also by assets not used to perform its essential functions. Decisions about the kind of secured debt are approved by the MoF.

The bankruptcy law prevents bankruptcy proceedings against LGs, but allows bankruptcy proceedings against their subsidiaries.

Immediate reaction to COVID-19

With the appearance of the first COVID patient in March 2020, Bosnia and Herzegovina federal government declared a state of emergency throughout the country. The two-state entities and the Brcko District adopted special laws that were binding on the municipalities in their territory. While the FB&H and the Brčko District have enacted the Law on Mitigation of Negative Consequences, the RS entity has taken a number of decisions to address certain pandemic-related issues. The most important decisions of the entity authorities that affect the municipalities were related to the postponement of the payment of taxes and fees for 2019 due in 2020, and in the FB&H, the decision not to pay the advance income tax payment. The FB&H planned a rebalancing budget assistance to municipal budgets due to the fall in their revenues.

All in all, authorities at the entity levels have not changed LG laws, or rules on fiscal discipline or fiscal status. Although the Coronavirus pandemic significantly affected the economic activity in Bosnia and Herzegovina and, thus, the municipal budgets, a significant part of the municipalities did not rebalance their budgets for 2020. In other words, the central government did not provide extraordinary powers to municipalities which, therefore, needed to act within the same fiscal rules in place before the pandemic arose.

Revenue structure

Understanding vulnerability before COVID-19

Revenue from indirect taxes, represented mainly by value added tax (VAT), constitutes the dominant share of tax revenues. They are collected by the central level and then divided among the State, the entities (RS and FB&H), and the Brčko District. Allocation of indirect taxes within each entity is regulated by entities' law. Indirect tax rates are determined at the State level and LGs do not have any influence on the basis or rate of indirect taxes, although these taxes in the most LGs represent dominant revenues.

In RS, 24% of indirect taxes belong to municipalities, while this percentage decreases to 8.4% in FB&H. These revenues are collected by the central level and then divided among the State, the entities, and the Brčko District according to a methodology provided by law, on the basis of population, jurisdiction area, number of pupils in primary education, and level of economic development. Indirect tax rates are determined at the State level and LGs do not have any influence on the basis or rate of indirect taxes, although these taxes in most LGs represent dominant revenues.

In addition to indirect taxes, LGs share the following shared taxes with the central level of government: personal income tax, corporate income tax, payroll tax, rental income from land owned by the central government, concession fees granted by the central government, and water fees.

The revenues that belong entirely to the LG are property tax, fines, municipal administrative fees, utility taxes, special water charges (water protection fees), municipal fees for the use of natural and other goods of general interest, tax on gambling winnings, residence taxes, concession fees for assignment for concessions awarded by LG, other income, such as grants, transfers, and revenues generated by performing regular and supplementary activities in accordance with the law.

The structure of LGs revenues differs as a result of the different distribution of revenues between the entity and local levels. Thus, in all RS municipalities, the share of indirect taxes is over 50%, while this percentage in the FB&H is on average 30% (Local Government Initiative, 2018).

Non-tax revenues like fees, charges, and revenues from the provision of public services are under the direct control of the municipality. The amount of these revenues in local budget depends on the rate for individual fees, as well as on the development of the economy and natural resources of the municipality. Municipalities that are developing rapidly generate a significant part of the fees from the arrangement of the city construction land, utility fees, and leases. On the other hand, a large number of small municipalities that have significant natural resources generate a significant share of revenues from concessions, fees for forests and water, which can make up to 45% of the total budget revenue. It can be said that in addition to revenues from indirect taxes, which is significant revenue in the budget of all municipalities, the structure of other revenues does not have a defined pattern and differs from municipality to municipality. According to Jusufbašić (2011), LGs have a weak own source of financing, although they are considered the closest government level to citizens and provide most public services.

Based on the Law on Local Self-Government in RS, the distribution of revenues to municipalities depends on their level of development.

LGs are subdivided into four categories according to their development status and potential as (a) developed, (b) medium developed, (c) underdeveloped, and (d) extremely underdeveloped municipalities. Criteria for determining the degree of development are adopted every three years. Through equalisation measures, the RS provides special support to financially underdeveloped and extremely underdeveloped units of local self-government, in order to reduce differences in the level of development and financial burden in the exercise of competences. In addition, other grants cover specific additional areas, such as small and medium enterprises, agriculture, environment, infrastructure, etc. (Council of Europe, 2019). In the FB&H, there is neither a formal, legal obligation nor a formalised equalisation system. Nevertheless, the share of transfers from the central government to municipal budgets in the RS is up to 8% mostly to underdeveloped municipalities, while in FB&H, this percentage is 20%.

Immediate reaction to COVID-19

Measures taken by Bosnia and Herzegovina governments in early March 2020 to prevent the spread of the Coronavirus have had a significant impact on the economy and, therefore, the GDP fell by 4.3% in 2020 compared to the previous year. In addition to health measures, it was forbidden to perform activities to all entities engaged in retail, except for pharmacies and supermarkets, while the work of other economic entities was limited. All these measures directly affected the reduction of spending and, thus, the reduction of revenues from VAT, which, as stated, is the most significant revenue in local budgets. In March, the decline in VAT revenues was 23% compared to the same period last year, while the decline in April reached 31% (Poljašević et al., 2020).

Furthermore, the decline in municipal revenues was influenced by both the economic measures of the central government and the measures adopted by cantons and the municipalities themselves. The postponement of the payment of personal income tax and corporate profit tax from March to the second half of the year affected budget liquidity, while the ban on performing activities affected the reduction of revenues of municipal institutions based on services they provide, such as kindergartens, museums, theatres, and other municipal services. In order to help the economy overcome the period of the ban on performing activities, some municipalities in RS made decisions not to collect rent, utility and other taxes, and municipal fees, while in FB&H, these decisions were adopted at the level of cantons.

Already in April 2020, the International Monetary Fund – IMF had approved €333 million to help Bosnia and Herzegovina to meet an urgent balance-of-payments need. About €65 million of these funds were distributed to the cantons and municipalities. In the FB&H, these funds allocated to cantons and municipalities are primarily intended to reimburse the costs incurred by municipalities by providing certain financial assistance to private companies. In the RS, a Compensation Fund for the remediation of the consequences caused by the Coronavirus has been established, and €15 million (17% of total Fund and 4.5% of budget revenues of all LGs) is intended for LGs. The distribution of these funds is the level of impact of the crisis on local finances and the level of economic development of the municipality, with special attention to underdeveloped LGs.

In the RS, the Republic of Srpska Investment-Development Bank (IRBRS) has announced a call for grants and financing related to projects of integrated and sustainable local development. LGs can borrow from an IRBRS for infrastructure projects, refinancing current obligations, and payment of tax obligations; furthermore, a lower interest rate applies to undeveloped LGs.

Although the budgets of LGs have been significantly affected by the pandemic crisis, there is no systematic assistance from the central government to the municipalities, leaving them alone to solve their own financial problems. During the immediate aftermath, not only the central government did not change the regulations related to debt and borrowing and the other regulations governing local finances, but also no specific extraordinary grants were allocated to LGs.

Expenditure structure

Understanding vulnerability before COVID-19

The largest share of LGs' total expenditures is attributable to the salary of their employees. After this are transfers and remittances, expenditure on consumption of goods and services, and social protection remittances. Salary expenditures vary among LGs and range from 31% to 50% of total expenditures, which is not surprising since 28% of the total number of employees in Bosnia and Herzegovina was employed in the public sector in 2020.

Although the cost structure varies between municipalities, most costs are fixed and very difficult to change in the short-term. For example, the cost of using goods and services is determined by the structure of services provided by municipalities to citizens, wages are determined by labour laws, social protection remittances are also determined by social security laws and are often prescribed by the central government.

Furthermore, LGs in Bosnia and Herzegovina have an obligation under the statute to provide water, heating, utility, and other services to citizens. For these purposes, LGs founded utility companies and transferred the infrastructure assets to them for management without ownership. As a result, LGs have significant investments and expenditures in upgrading their public utility infrastructure and often financially support utility companies.

Immediate reaction to COVID-19

The pandemic affected the level of LG expenditures differently; while there was a significant increase in some expenditures, others decreased due to the circumstances in which LGs operated. Also, the decisions of both the central government and LGs influenced the change in the structure and amount of expenditure. The travel ban has resulted in a reduction in travel, conference, and seminar expenditures, but the share of these expenditures in the total expenditures of most LGs is negligible. On the other hand, the need for constant disinfection in facilities, street washing, and the distribution of hygiene materials to vulnerable groups of the population has increased the cost of materials. In addition to these influences, LGs have made individual decisions to help the population and the economy. These aids mainly related to the free delivery of food and medicine to elderly citizens who were forbidden to leave their homes, payment of utilities to socially disadvantaged families, distribution of free agricultural packages as support of spring sowing, subsidising interest and creating conditions for more favourable lending, grant funds for artisans who are extremely affected by the crisis, and grant funds for industrial protection. At the same time, there was a reduction in other expenditures, primarily subsidies, transfers, and grants to individuals and organisations.

However, the largest expenditure items remained at the same level since the salaries of workers in municipalities did not change and a large number of projects and services that municipalities had planned in their 2020 budgets had already started at the beginning of the year with contracts signed with suppliers. As a result, in most municipalities, total expenditures changed slightly compared to those planned at the beginning of 2020.

Vulnerability outlook

Understanding vulnerability before COVID-19

Budget planning at the LG level begins in July of the previous year. On the one hand, revenues from indirect taxes are planned by the Indirect Taxation Authority on the basis of projected GDP growth, and the information is submitted to the central government and LGs. The Department of Macroeconomic Planning within the MoF plans direct revenues shared between the central government and LGs, while revenues directly influenced by municipalities are forecast based on historical data, GDP growth, and expected inflation and adjusted for forecasts of economic activity in the municipality. On the other hand, most budget expenditures have a fixed character such as employee salaries, social benefits, loan repayments, and ongoing investment expenditures. Based on the confrontation of the above categories, a decision is made on borrowing if the expenditures are higher than the receipts in order to balance the budget. Usually, historical data are used for forecast, while no econometric analyses are usually applied to consider medium-long term trends for costs and revenues.

In Bosnia and Herzegovina, there is no set of indicators used to monitor the vulnerability of LGs, with the exception of the state of indebtedness and the possibility of debt repayment. The next problem with monitoring the financial situation is the public unavailability of financial reports and budget execution reports. In the RS, municipalities are obliged to submit annual financial reports to the Data Processing Agency as well as to the Ministry of Finance (MoF), while periodic and annual reporting on budget execution is submitted to the MoF. In addition to the MoF, the RS established a Fiscal Council in 2017 whose role is to analyse and verify macroeconomic and fiscal assumptions and projections used in drafting government documents, provide an independent and credible assessment of economic policy, assess basic fiscal risks, and likelihood that governments will meet its targets in the future, assesses the extent to which fiscal targets have been met and verifies that fiscal rules have been met.

Local and central governments are obliged to provide the Fiscal Council with information on the total amount of arrears from the previous year, an overview of the level of indebtedness, guarantees given, data on concluded contracts or litigation, as well as an overview of potential risks in individual concluded contracts or possible litigation which can lead to unplanned obligations. In case LGs have outstanding liabilities from the previous period, they submit to the Fiscal Council a plan for settling liabilities with the indicated sources from which the liabilities will be settled, deadlines and dynamics of settlement, and an explanation of the reasons that led to the current situation. In order to increase fiscal responsibility, heads of LGs have to sign the Statement of Fiscal Responsibility for the purposeful and legal spending of funds and the efficiency and successful functioning of the system of financial internal control.

In the FB&H, the periodic and annual reports on budget execution as well as financial reports are submitted to the cantons and the consolidated report is submitted by the cantons to the MoF. Therefore, entity-level MoFs monitor local finances and consolidate data at the LGs at the entity level. There is no single database of financial and budget reports of municipalities at the level of Bosnia and Herzegovina, so no institution deals with monitoring and public disclosure of data on the finances of local authorities at the level of Bosnia and Herzegovina.

In RS, the overall financial situation of LGs is considered satisfactory (Council of Europe, 2019). No information is available for FB&H. In 2017, the LGs achieved a surplus of €16 million (4.8% of budget revenues of all LGs), which means that expenditures were reimbursed from revenues and capital investments were financed. At the same time, the unallocated surplus was €13 million as a result of excess revenues and inflows in relation to expenditures, capital investments, and loan payments. In 2018, the situation worsened slightly but was still considered satisfactory with an overall surplus of €1 million, with 17 LGs suffering budget deficits and a total surplus of €5 million.

All in all, three categories of municipalities could be distinguished before the pandemic arose, according to their budgetary situation: cities and large LGs which had stable budgets but sometimes problems with over-investments; smaller LGs which often have problems on the revenue side; and small LGs with natural resources (mining, water, forest), which permits budgetary stability, together with other resources.

At the end of 2019, the debt of LGs in Bosnia and Herzegovina was €208 million (3.9% of GDP) with a decrease from the previous year of €211.50 million. External debt, i.e. the debt owed to foreign creditors, was 6% of total LGs debt, while internal debt was 94% and represented 12% of the total internal public debt of Bosnia and Herzegovina (Ministarstvo finansija i trezora Bosne i Hercegovine, 2019). LGs external debt increased by +80% in the 2014–2018 periods and most of this debt was related to infrastructure investments.

Immediate reaction to COVID-19

According to an NALAS (2020) survey conducted in local communities in Sought-Eastern Europe (SEE) during the lockdown (March–June 2020), local revenues were severely hit: in 81% of LGs, own revenues decreased by more than 20% in annual terms; at the same time, also intergovernmental transfers fell for 65% of SEE LGs. In Bosnia and Herzegovina, the COVID-19 pandemic began in March, when the budgets for 2020 had already been adopted, while at the same time, the reports on the execution of the budget for 2019 were still being prepared. Since the local elections in Bosnia and Herzegovina would be held in October 2020, the planned capital investments for the 2020 fiscal year were five times higher than the previous one, while at the beginning of the year significant capital investments began and contracts were signed with contractors. While the pandemic crisis caused a decline in revenues, most LGs aimed to leave expenditures almost at the same level, despite some differences in their structure.

In general, in Bosnia and Herzegovina, the least affected by the crisis were municipalities that had dominant indirect taxes and fees in their revenue structure based on the use of natural resources, because these economic entities did not reduce their work capacity. The largest municipalities were most affected because the share of their own revenues in the budget was dominant, as well as the municipalities that are known as tourist destinations. Only in RS information on infra-annual budget execution was available, allowing some assessment of the level of LG vulnerability. According to the reports on budget execution for the first half of 2020, the realised tax revenues were 10% lower compared to the previous year with income and profit tax 82% lower, property tax 61% lower, while VAT only 7% lower. At the same time, non-tax revenues were 8% lower than the previous year. Although only 22% of the planned capital investments were realised, this amount was higher by 77% than the previous year. Since the planned capital investments could not be financed from their own sources, LGs planned to borrow almost the entire amount of the capital investment, and by the end of June 2020, they had borrowed 103% of the planned amount. No assessment of how the pandemic impacted on LGs finances was in place in the FB&H.

Final remarks

The existence of two entities and districts in Bosnia and Herzegovina that have their own laws on the functioning and financing of LGs has conditioned the different financial conditions of LGs. Common to all LGs, is that in the immediate outbreak, these governments have given priority to safeguarding citizens' health and lives and helping those most affected by the lockdown. Other than the consequences of lockdown, most recovery measures focused on the local economy and social protection.

Occupied with problems at the state entity level, the state entity governments paid little attention to LGs and their financial problems. The FB&H government redirected part of the IMF loan to the cantons, while further distribution to municipalities depended on each canton individually. In the RS, a small part of the funds from the Compensation Fund is directed to municipalities without clear criteria for allocating transfers.

Although it is clear that the 2020 budgets have not been realised as planned, only a small number of municipalities have rebalanced their budgets, although it is a legal obligation. Since revenues have not been realised as planned, it would have been necessary to verify the sources for budget expenditures. LGs that rebalanced missing funds with loans or surpluses from previous years managed to rebalance their budgets. For LGs that failed to rebalance their budgets, deficits have inevitably emerged.

Governments at the central level have not taken any action to assess and monitor the situation in LGs, change the provisions concerning LG financial vulnerability, and have mostly left LGs to solve on their own the problems induced by the pandemic.

6 Germany

René Geissler

Country profile: Germany

Population	83.0 million inhabitants (2019)
Government system	Federal state and parliamentary democracy
Territorial organisation	Three tiers, federal level (*Bund*), states (*Länder*) and city states (*Stadtstaaten*), and local governments, i.e. counties (*Kreise*) and municipalities (*Gemeinden*)
Number of LGs	11,087 municipalities and 295 counties (2019)
LG average size	7,488 inhabitants (municipalities); 54% of municipalities have fewer than 2,000 inhabitants

Sources: OECD/UCLG (2019); Federal Office of Statistics, Germany, https://www.destatis.de/EN/Themes/Countries-Regions/Regional-Statistics/_node.html.

Introduction

Germany is a federal state with 13 regional and three city states (Geissler, 2019, p. 102). Local governments (LGs) are part and subject of the states. Local levels in all states consist primarily of municipalities and counties. Among about 11,000 municipalities, 103 are independent cities, meaning, they are not subordinated to a county and deliver as county as municipal services. The remaining municipalities are part of one of the 295 German counties. Hence, there are three types of LGs in every state: municipalities, independent cities, and counties. In most of the states, there are administrative partnerships (*Verwaltungsgemeinschaft*) of smaller municipalities within a county: Small municipalities remain autonomous legally, politically, and in deciding their budgets, but delegate the execution of most of their functions to such administrative partnerships. In five out of 13 states, there are associations of counties and cities with county rights too (*höherer Kommunalverband*). Their members delegate particular functions, such as welfare, to such associations in order to reach higher effectiveness. Hence, there are great differences in local structures

DOI: 10.4324/9781003274278-6

and number of inhabitants across jurisdictions. During the last decades, different approaches to restructure the local level of government and reduce the number of counties and municipalities have been implemented so that the number of LGs and their average population differ across states.

Administrative structure and fiscal rules

Understanding vulnerability before COVID-19

The German administrative system is quite complex. In most cases, basic legal principles are set at the federal level and complemented by state law. There is hardly any essential service autonomously delivered by LGs on their own. In contrast, state and federal interferences in local services, referring to regulation or funding, have increased especially after the 2008 financial crisis. The complexity of local finance has risen and is an ongoing political issue.

Local fiscal autonomy is established by the constitution and regulated by state law (Geissler, 2019, p. 109). In every state, LGs are obliged to adhere to the balanced budget rule. Debt is restricted to fund capital spending and supervisory agencies have to approve it before the fiscal year starts. Short-term credits are restricted to ensure liquidity needs. There is no bankruptcy regulation for municipalities, but an implicit bailout expectation by the states. Different forms of bailouts have grown remarkably in the aftermath of the financial crisis (Person and Geissler, 2021). Thus, every LG is creditworthy and benefits from minimal interest rates.

There is an established and old system of fiscal oversight, implemented by the states via the Ministry of Interior or the counties. Before the end of the preceding year, every LG has to hand in its budget plan to the supervisory body for verifying its consistency with fiscal rules. If rules are broken, supervisory bodies enjoy a range of sanctioning instruments, for example rejecting budget proposals, neglecting credit approvals, enforcing cutback programs, up to taking over local administrations.

Fiscal rules and fiscal regulations are strict so as to prevent budget crises and to discipline local budgeting. Fiscal supervision plays a relevant role in budgeting and local measures because of fiscal stress. However, it needs to be considered that, although the institutional setting is very similar among German states, its implementation differs and, thus, local budgeting as well (Person and Geissler, 2021).

Immediate aftermath of COVID-19

The pandemic did not have any impact on local administrative structures. During the last decade, some states were characterised by intensified political debate on restructuring the local level. However, due to public and local level opposition, any reforming attempts failed once and for all before COVID-19.

Although the federal government and the states implemented some minor changes and temporarily took over the regulation of some activities to improve effectiveness also at the local level, the pandemic did not have major impacts on local functions, too. There have been attempts by the federal level to regulate the pandemic policies of the states and of local health authorities, such as dealing with the closure of schools, kindergarten, or shops, in order to have a common national approach against COVID-19. Given the complex constitutional setting of German federalism, those federal attempts did not pay off in the short-term but are expected to go on in the years to come.

When as a consequence of COVID-19 the recession spread, concerns emerged about the impact of local fiscal rules on local functionality. Usually, LGs have to react to a decline in revenue or an unplanned demand in spending with spending freezes, supplementary budgets or cutbacks. The total amount of liquidity loans, which might be necessary in such a context, needs to be approved by supervisory bodies to be increased within a budget year. Such fiscal rules could cause dramatic consequences on the functionality of LGs as they require bureaucratic efforts, consume valuable time, and slow down crisis reactions.

Consequentially, those fiscal rules were suspended in the majority of states after the beginning of COVID-19. In addition, some states suspended the balanced budget requirement for the upcoming budgeting process and allowed LGs to decide to run unbalanced budgets. This state reaction was unique and follows the clear intention to keep LGs liquid and avoid any unnecessary financial restrain.

Revenue structure

Understanding vulnerability before COVID-19

By federal and state constitution, LGs are granted fiscal autonomy, that is they can raise local taxes and have budgeting rights.

Higher-level grants and local taxes make up for equal shares of LG revenues (Geissler, 2019, p. 103). In addition, there is a range of charges and user fees for particular services (e.g. utilities and kindergartens).

The structure and amount of grants is decided by the states and, hence, they differ widely among them. The most relevant kind of grants are unconditional grants calculated based on the number of inhabitants, fiscal capacity, and fiscal need (*Schlüsselzuweisung*). Due to some state court decisions, the relevance of state reimbursements for services transferred to the local level is rising.

Counties do not enjoy taxation rights, but levy contributions through their municipalities. Municipalities and independent cities receive shares of the general income tax as well as the value-added tax, whose tax rates are set at the federal level. Additionally, municipalities levy property taxes and business taxes at rates decided independently.

Business taxes are the most relevant local tax and generate a fifth of municipal revenues. They are based mostly on business profits and, because of the positive economic development, there has been a robust growth in business tax revenue over the past years (about 28% within the period from 2014 to 2018). This makes business taxes volatile because of the very close link among business taxes, the local economic structure, and the business cycle. One specific feature of business taxes is an interim payment based on past payments. In case of worsening economic conditions, companies can cut those interim payments, and this is what is crucial for the financial vulnerability of LGs.

The second relevant local taxes are property taxes, which have also experienced a robust growth trend, but as a consequence of higher tax rates (about 3% annually). There has not been a revaluation of property values for decades. The property tax system has been recently revised and results are still unknown.

Therefore, municipalities enjoy a high degree of autonomy with regard to tax rates. Nonetheless, there is some state influence to guarantee fiscal equalisation: To avoid tax competition and a race to the bottom, municipalities having tax rates below a certain level are disadvantaged in the distribution of general grants.

In recent years, widening disparities in tax rates have been observed among municipalities. Municipalities facing budget crises or benefitting from conditional bailouts had to raise their rates, especially regarding property taxes. As an example, the city of Oberhausen in North Rhine-Westphalia, experiencing long-term structural change and fiscal stress, had to set a rate for business tax of 20%. Only a few miles away in the same state, the city of Monheim, implementing a dumping strategy, levied a 10% business tax. Eventually, an adverse situation developed, where weaker municipalities with less infrastructure and lower service levels have higher tax rates than stronger ones.

Overall, the composition of local revenues follows LGs' economic strength due to the major impact of business taxes. However, in every state, there is an individual municipal financial equalisation system. Most states base the level of redistribution of revenues at least partly on the socioeconomic structure of the municipalities and their concomitant needs. In most states, there are tax redistributions at the local level, so that richer municipalities have to transfer shares of revenue to poorer ones. With growing economic disparities, redistribution amongst municipalities has become more relevant.

Immediate aftermath of COVID-19

COVID-19 hit local budgets both in terms of revenue as well as expenditure (Freier and Geissler, 2020). It induced a large economic crisis: Companies incurred such hardship nationwide that business tax revenue was expected to drop by about 20% in 2020–2021. As the labor market and consumption suffered, the local share of personal income tax and VAT was expected to drop, too. With the shutdown of local services, there has been a loss of user charges. The local service revenue which has been most affected is kindergarten fees, but revenues from cultural institutions, sports or public transport have suffered shortfalls, too.

One relevant federal decision was the possibility for companies to cut business tax interim payments and to send employees on short-term work, reducing their working hours. The former decision had a direct impact on local tax revenues, the latter one reduced wages and personal income tax.

The decline of business taxes hit LGs the hardest in the second quarter of 2020 when the first lockdown was in place. As an example, municipalities of Germany's largest state North Rhine-Westphalia suffered a 40% loss in business tax revenue compared to the previous year.

Against this background, the federal government and the states decided and implemented a historic program of financial support. The most relevant one was the reimbursement of business tax losses in 2020, jointly funded by the federal and state governments. The amount of tax reimbursements were calculated on the basis of the spring GDP forecast and unaffected by real developments. This reimbursement was paid off in 2020 to stabilise budgets in that financial year and to avoid major deficits.

Actually, statistics show an escalation of liquidity loans in the fall of 2020, mirroring losses in revenue and unplanned spending. By the end of the year, using state and federal aid, those amounts were recovered.

A second essential support was the permanently rise of the reimbursement of welfare-housing costs, funded at federal level. This measure refers to long-term claims by LGs and backed economically weak cities in particular. In addition, there were numerous further sector-specific supports for example public transport, hospitals, local health offices, or cultural institutions. Federal and state-level reimbursed specific health services, too.

As the 13 states can individually decide on financial measures, there has been a great variance among the financial policies implemented across Germany. Few states reacted to COVID-19 with emergency grants distributed based on population size to cover unforeseeable spending. Other ones reimbursed losses of user charges (in particular kindergarten). One specific concern lies in state's fiscal equalisation schemes. Due to losses in state's tax revenues, those grants will decline in the upcoming years. Hence, the measures and extent of financial support have varied among states and fiscal impacts have differed too as economic structure, local functions and funding are different.

Expenditure structure

Understanding vulnerability before COVID-19

LGs are in charge of a wide range of services, mostly devolved by state law such as social protection, education, local economic affairs, recreation, culture, environmental protection, housing, and public safety (Geissler, 2019, pp. 105–106). The largest (and growing) share of expenditures is welfare services such as kindergarten, social benefits, and refugees. Such costs have proved to be highly dynamic over time. For example, spending for kindergarten, following a legal claim from parents, more than doubled within the ten years from 2010 to 2020 from 17 billion to 40 billion euros. This is the major reason why the local share of general government expenditure rose.

The states set the precise structure and range of services; consequently, there is a substantial variation across Germany. Most significant differences exist in welfare services, which have a direct impact on local budgets. For example, LGs in North Rhine-Westphalia and Hesse have to deliver services for disabled people, whereas elsewhere this is a state function. LGs, which are in charge to deliver a broader range of welfare services, bear higher risks of underfunded mandates and unbalanced budgets. The long-term and strong rise in welfare spending is an ongoing issue for those LGs. During the last decade, this issue could only be kept under control by the strong growth in tax revenues and larger transfers from the federal level. Thus, local budgets were highly vulnerable to economic downturns and cuts in federal grants.

LGs also play a role in the provision of health services. For example, cities and counties run the local health services related to the protection from a pandemic and the supervision of sanitation efforts. As they are rare occurrences, no standards for staffing and performance were developed, so that LGs had silently neglected those services for many years. About one-quarter of German hospitals are owned locally. This number has been shrinking for many years, because of high capital demands and financial risks. One out of eight public hospitals was closed from 2010 to 2019.

LGs implement the majority of public investments with the total amount of local capital spending rising by more than 60% from 2012 to 2019. This trend was also fostered by special federal grants meant to stimulate economic growth, to push expansion of kindergarten and schools, and to bridge the shortfalls of poorer LGs. Nonetheless, the share of capital spending on total local spending shrank from 17% in 2000 to 10% in 2016, starting a debate on investment backlog. For example, regarding education, LGs are responsible for school infrastructure and the drop in investments created rising pressure and a backlog in renovations and new infrastructures.

In such a dynamic context there are significant disparities among municipalities when it comes to expenditure by functions: Economically weaker cities show proportionally higher spending levels for welfare and lower ones for capital spending.

Immediate aftermath of COVID-19

On the expenditure side of local budgets, the pandemic has affected most functions in one way or another (Freier and Geissler, 2020, p. 5). The most direct impact was on local health services, as they are in charge of monitoring and slowing down the spreading of COVID-19 and of assessing sanitation efforts. In the middle term, LGs expected also rise in social spending due to growing unemployment (Henneke, 2020, p. 147). In general, the complexity of many local services has grown and so did their costs. For example, LGs needed ad hoc digitalisation to enable remote working, while the intensity of local police services has risen, as did waste disposal. Moreover, running schools and kindergartens became more demanding due to sanitation requirements. LGs had to come up with backup solutions for preparing many public services for future lockdowns, even though such spending was rather low, fragmented, and hard to measure.

Although some local services closed or experienced declines in workload, LGs did not reduce employees working hours so as not to reduce wages.

Some states reacted with emergency grants to cover additional and unforeseeable expenditures, while the federal government has started programs to support local health services and digitalisation. Both the federal government and the states claim they intend to shield local budgets from COVID-19 and to avoid distortions in local expenditures.

Finally, at the federal level, it was decided to fund major COVID driven expenses such as testing and vaccination. As local health services proved insufficient to cope with COVID-19 demands, the central government started a midterm support program to extend those local capacities. However, even with such federal grants, it is expected that local expenditures will rise.

Vulnerability outlook

Understanding vulnerability before COVID-19

There was no systematic risk assessment of the financial vulnerability of LGs be it at federal or state level. States delivered forecasts for tax revenues as one fundamental aspect of local budget planning. There is no general discussion or toolbox for vulnerability scenarios at local level, too. At most, rich cities, which depend heavily on business taxes, keep a close eye on their major local companies to assess future tax revenues. However, as there is an extensive fiscal equalisation, there was little need for a local assessment of financial risks.

Immediate aftermath of COVID-19

Experts have foreseen a major decline in tax revenue, which, because of business taxes, would hit rich cities harder than poorer ones (Freier and Geissler, 2020). Surveys among local experts foreseen a dramatic worsening in the overall financial situation across the board (Brand et al., 2020).

Those declines were already measurable by mid-2020. There was no expectation of a fast and comprehensive economic recovery. In addition, COVID-19 hit the German economy in a period of stagnation while facing large structural changes concerning the automotive sector, digitalisation efforts, and export reconsiderations. As a consequence, tax revenues were expected to remain on a lower growth path than before.

However, even without the federal and state programs, the financial situation of LGs was rather sound before COVID-19. Local revenues saw a multi-annual strong growth, liquidity loans decreased significantly, as well as the share of LGs experiencing a budgetary crisis. Many LGs built up essential deposits during the last economically strong years. As an example, the total reserve funds of Bavarian LGs can cover the business tax revenues for two years. However, poorer LGs did not have the possibility to build such reserves, as they did not generate surpluses. Those cities were still burdened by short-term credits, which would have risen again in the short term.

For the time being by the end of 2020, loosening of fiscal rules and generous state and federal support bridged financial shortfalls and there was no need for local cutback measures. Federal and state financial support should be able to cover most, but not all, short-term impacts. This positive situation might change in the next years when the reimbursement of business tax runs out. In this case, fiscal stress may affect many parts of LGs. Usual reactions are cuts in capital spending, tax raises, pressures on human resource expenditures and, in general, a loss of fiscal autonomy. Therefore, a financial crisis may have been simply postponed and COVID-19 has not contributed to strengthen the assessment of financial vulnerability at the local level.

Final remarks

COVID-19 caused an important economic recession. It hit an economy, which found itself in stagnation with a cloudy outlook after a decade of strong growth. Many LGs had improved their financial situation over the previous years, but some showed ongoing fiscal stress as their finances were stretched too far.

Local rules and structures, as well as revenues and functions, are state issues and differ among states and types of LGs. Local revenue structure has always been volatile to business cycles due to the important role played by business taxes. LGs perform services, which have been crucial during the pandemic, such as health services, unemployment benefits, and kindergartens.

COVID-19 meant for LGs a decline in business tax revenue, higher demands in health service, and more complexity for school and kindergarten infrastructure. The federal government and the states reacted soon enough with financial support, in particular refunding business tax losses. This generous support is explained by the political will to shield local budgets and to keep LGs functioning during the crisis. This policy means a remarkable change in comparison to the financial crisis ten years before when state and federal level accepted large local deficits. As a consequence of COVID-19, the local dependence on federal transfers has grown, along with a further increase in federal fiscal interdependence.

In addition, the states and federal government used an emergency clause to suspend their debt brake rule, allowing to finance their tremendous support. The suspension of local public fiscal rules by some states was a remarkable step, but probably unnecessary given state and federal financial aid. However, most of this support is limited to this initial phase, so fiscal stress is expected to grow in the coming years.

7 Italy

Emanuele Padovani and Silvia Iacuzzi

Country profile: Italy

Population	60.4 million inhabitants (2019)
Government system	Unitary state and parliamentary democracy
Territorial organisation	Three tiers, central state, regions (*regioni*) and local governments composed of municipalities (*comuni*), provinces (*province*)*, metropolitan cities (*cittm metropolitane*)* and unions of municipalities (*unioni di comuni*)* (* = second-tiers or intermediate local governments)
Number of LGs	7,904 municipalities, 107 provinces and metropolitan cities, 565 unions of municipalities (2021)
LG average size	7,615 inhabitants (municipalities); 44% of municipalities have fewer than 2,000 inhabitants

Sources: OECD/UCLG (2019); ISTAT - National Statistic Office, Italy, https://www.istat.it/it/archivio/216271

Introduction

Italy is a unitary country with a highly regionalised structure (Bettoni, 2017, p. 103). It is organised in three tiers of governments: central state, regions (*regioni*), and local governments (LGs) level that consists of municipalities (*comuni*), provinces (*province*), metropolitan cities (*città metropolitane*), and unions of municipalities (*unioni di comuni*). Local self-government is a constitutionally enshrined right (Bespalova and Andersen, 2013). Yet, only regions and municipalities enjoy constitutionally assured revenue and expenditure autonomy (article 119, Italian Constitution) with all other levels playing mainly administrative and service provision functions. Provinces, metropolitan cities, and unions of municipalities are second tiers or intermediate LGs whose aim is to achieve economies of scale, increasing the efficiency of public service provision, and delivering services which may not be possible for municipalities.

DOI: 10.4324/9781003274278-7

The 7,926 municipalities represent the local authorities closest to the citizens. Seventy percent of them have fewer than 5,000 inhabitants and the average population is just above 7,500 inhabitants, depicting a highly fragmented setting. In general, municipal responsibilities include town planning, building and commercial permits, social housing, local (municipal) police, public transport and roads, water and waste management, education (pre and primary school buildings), social services, local economic development, recreation and culture, etc. (OECD/UCLG, 2019).

Administrative structure and fiscal rules

Understanding vulnerability before COVID-19

There are three main fiscal rules that affect the financial management of municipalities: the deficit golden rule, bankruptcy procedures, and debt ceilings. First, the constitution foresees that LGs can incur deficits only for investment purposes (Vandelli, 2012, p. 355; Mostacci, 2016, p. 198;). Since 2016, there is only one unique budget balance target for all LGs calculated on an accrual basis (Camera dei deputati, 2018).

Second, acquiring new debt is subject to more specific restrictions than the possibility to borrow money only for investments. Quantitative limits are imposed on borrowing according to annual revenues and municipalities can take on new debt only if the annual expenses for interests (of any form of past, new debt or guarantee) do not exceed a specific proportion of current revenues, now set at 10% of the second to last previous fiscal year.

Third, Italian municipalities (and LGs in general) are subject to bankruptcy procedures (Ambrosanio et al. 2016, p. 233; Padovani et al. 2018, p. 6). Different from a state takeover but similarly to the private sector, a bankruptcy procedure refers to that situation where insolvency is declared by the council or ascertained by the Court of Auditors (the highest external auditor body), and creditors are paid by clearance of assets and credits. The law provides three types of financial distress: bankruptcy, the most severe default level (*dissesto*); pre-default (*predissesto*), an intermediate level which is a sort of condition detected by specific index thresholds in which the LG is subjected to a series of central government continuous checks; and imbalance, the least acute level that occurs in the rebalancing procedure (*procedura di riequilibrio*). An LG is considered to be bankrupt (*dissesto*) when (a) it is not able to continue its functions and essential services (i.e. service insolvency) or (b) it cannot pay creditors with regular resources (i.e. financial insolvency). Between 1989 and 2013, only 495 provincial and municipal governments, most of them in the South of Italy, were affected by severe fiscal distress. But just six years after the financial crisis, between 2012 and 2017, 127 municipal and provincial governments experienced the *dissesto* procedure and 196 the *procedura di riequilibrio*. According to Ambrosanio et al. (2016, p. 233), the result of this "schizophrenic procedurals" (*dissesto* versus *procedura di riequilibrio*) is that several municipalities and provinces, especially in the South, are still on the verge of bankruptcy and have had a history of bailouts, which are decided at the political level.

Immediate aftermath of COVID-19

The first decisions by the central government to face the COVID-19 pandemic were taken with specific decree laws in March (the so-called "Cure Italy decree") and May ("Relaunch decree"). The specific provisions that affected the financial management of municipalities can be grouped into four types: (1) postponement of several revenue collection deadlines during the lockdown period, (2) cash advances, (3) relief grants in view of local taxes and fees-related revenues reduction, and (4) postponement of capital instalment of mortgages.

While these can be considered extraordinary measures to tackle the financial shock caused by the pandemic, no extraordinary powers were devolved to municipalities. In particular, municipalities had to balance their budget, whose deadline for 2020 was first extended to the end of July and then to the end of October 2020 and cannot incur in current deficit spending to be financed by debt. Furthermore, while the national association of municipalities, ANCI, has specifically asked for a review of bankruptcy procedures (ANCI, 2020), they have remained the same and there currently is the risk that several municipalities declare bankruptcy.

All in all, there has been no change in the administrative structure and the fiscal rules. The central government has not devolved special powers to municipalities, which could, thus, react within their ordinary administrative and fiscal frameworks.

Revenue structure

Understanding vulnerability before COVID-19

Municipalities rely on transfers from other (mainly central and regional) governments, local taxes, and fees. Their revenue structure is quite different and based on their capability to raise local taxes and local fees, as well as the structure of their services. While on average, the dependency rate from other government levels is 29%, those municipalities belonging to wealthy areas, especially Northern Italy, enjoy an even lower dependency.

Those municipal governments below the national average, i.e. with lower capacity to raise their own taxes, are eligible for transfers (Mostacci, 2016, p. 198). Central government current transfers to municipalities consist exclusively of general-purpose equalisation grants, which are distributed subject to an equalisation mechanism that has been refined during the last ten years and considers expenditure needs as well as the fiscal capacity of a municipality. This equalisation mechanism is valid for municipalities falling into ordinary statute regions, while special statute regions in border areas can be subject to different provisions. Some earmarked grants, however, do exist even if they are limited, since they are basically banned by the Italian constitution. Hence, these transfers are provided from the central level to cushion regional disparities for economic development, social cohesion, natural disasters, etc.

The main source of tax revenue for municipalities are the municipal property tax (*IMU*), calculated on the basis of the cadastral value of the property in part defined by the central state, in part by the municipality; a surcharge on personal income tax (*Addizionale IRPEF*), where municipalities have some discretion on the tax rate; and the waste collection and disposal tax (*TARI*), calculated on the number of household members and the net living space of a residential property. Moreover, there is a municipal tax on building licenses and, especially in touristic municipalities, a tourist tax decided at the local level. Other residual revenues, but that can be determinant for each municipality's budget, stem from user charges and fees as well as from property income (OECD/UCLG, 2019), for example advertisement tax, kindergarten feeds, pre- and post-school fees, museum and theatre fees, elderly services fees, parking fees, occupation of public land tax, rentals, local police fines, and municipal enterprise revenues. With a few exceptions, these are fully decided at the local level.

Immediate aftermath of COVID-19

The central government has provided several measures that have influenced the revenue structure of municipalities. First, considering the shutdown of several economic sectors, it decided to postpone several revenue collection deadlines during the first lockdown period, which in Italy spanned from the beginning of March to the end of April 2020.

Second, considering the collapse of local revenues caused by tax collection postponements coupled with the reduction of fees due to partial or total stop to municipal services such as public transportation, kindergarten, pre- and post-school services, parking and ticketing for law enforcement, the central government provided cash advances to LGs. This intervention was intended to support the local economy by avoiding that municipalities would lack funds not only to provide fundamental services, but also to pay their personnel and suppliers. There were two main measures: (a) in May, a cash advance of 66% of regular grants (*Fondo di solidarietà comunale, FSC*), which covers about 7% of current expenditures plus debt instalments; (b) a bank overdraft facility (new debt) provided between June and July for a total amount of 12% of current expenditures plus debt instalments.

Third, with the May decree, the central government established several relief grants totalling another 7% of current expenditures plus debt instalments to contrast the net reduction of (accrued) local revenues that were expected to occur. In particular, to support some business activities, the central state enacted the cancellation of local revenues such as property tax to hotels, tourism tax, occupation of public land tax for bar and restaurants, summer camps fees and, at the same time, replaced them with specific relief grants for LGs. These new funds were distributed to municipalities on the basis not only of revenues reduction, but also on standard needs, i.e. an index that reflects the need for fundamental services required in each jurisdiction, minus any cost reductions that the municipality obtained.

There were, therefore, two major consequences on the revenue structure of municipalities: a slowdown of own revenue collection replaced by an increase of cash transfers from the central government on one hand and a replacement of own revenues with extraordinary relief grants on the other.

Expenditure structure

Understanding vulnerability before COVID-19

The structure of municipal expenditures varies widely across municipalities as it depends on which services are provided and how. Some municipal services, such as general administration, public and private buildings and infrastructures, environmental protection, social services, waste collection and disposal, public transportation, local police, are considered fundamental and, therefore, they are provided in all jurisdictions. Yet others, such as cultural events, sports and recreation, touristic services, just to name a few, depend on local needs, conditions, traditions, and so on. Similarly, provision settings may differ considerably due to the presence of municipal consortia (*unioni di comuni*) or municipal enterprises (*società participate*). In the latter cases, municipalities may not incur directly expenditures for services provided by other entities on their behalf.

On average, less than one-third of current revenues, 31%, is allocated to personnel and debt service (source: BDAP, Ministry of Economic and Finance), which are considered expenditures which have to be born and cannot be cancelled if needed be. While this is the prominent index of expenditure rigidity, it is widely recognised that this does not represent the whole picture. In fact, other current expenditures can be considered rigid (fixed maintenance contracts, fundamental service costs, etc.), as the municipality must bear them to provide minimum standards for delivering fundamental services.

Immediate aftermath of COVID-19

The pandemic had three different types of impact on current expenditures. First, more sanitisation of public spaces and offices and higher local police control during lockdowns have caused an increase in costs. Second, suspending many activities has led related services to stop and costs to reduce. For example, the closure of schools has caused school-related services, such as pre- and post-school services, school transportation, and school cafeterias to stop. The slowdowns of public transportation and the services for tourists (including utilities for tourists) should have resulted in further cost reductions. Third, social services have had a somewhat dual impact: On one hand, new social services have been implemented to face new needs (e.g. additional financial support to national measures and additional services, such as food and medicine delivery especially for seniors), on the other hand, certain social services (e.g. home visits) have not been carried out due to social distancing measures. A special regulation was issued by the central government to renegotiate the types of services to be provided within the same financial commitment, notwithstanding public tenders rules. No impacts were forecast on investments, at least in the 2020 fiscal year.

Furthermore, the central government level provided some measures to temporarily reduce rigid expenditures. In particular, specific regulations and agreements with banks and financial institutions offered the possibility to renegotiate mortgages so as to postpone one year repayment of the capital part of due instalments, representing at least 2.5% of current expenditures plus debt instalments.

Hence, municipalities explored a mix of possibilities with increases and reductions of expenditures, aiming at providing necessary services, while reducing them when possible, so as to comply with the current budget balance.

Vulnerability outlook

Understanding vulnerability before COVID-19

Traditionally in Italy, financial forecasts are approached using mainly a historic perspective at national, regional and municipal levels. Basically, the budget for the incoming year is mainly dealt with by adding inflation to current expenditures and then adjusting revenues accordingly. Capital expenditures and revenues are forecasted separately in relation to specific projects. In case of reorganisation of local taxes, overall revenues would then be adjusted so as to cover costs (Anessi-Pessina et al., 2012). No econometric analyses are usually applied at national, regional, or local level to consider medium-long term trends for costs and revenues.

LG financial vulnerability is measured using several indicators, of which the following can be considered the most important (Corte dei Conti, 2021): doubtful accounts receivable, off-balance debt, arrears (overdue debts). In order to avoid bankruptcy, municipalities often rely on window-dressing practices by counting even doubtful accounts receivable (*residui attivi*) as revenues to cover expenses. *Residui attivi* are uncollected sums (e.g. due payments for fines or tariffs) that the municipality promises to collect to balance the budget in the coming period. However, often a part of them does not materialise in the following period and municipalities keep on using them to balance the budget over and over again. This may keep oversight bodies at arm's length without solving the issue of ongoing deficits. Therefore, the Court of Auditors uses one indicator to evaluate fiscal health at local level the abnormal size of *residui attivi*, especially those that have arisen over many years for local revenues, since grants and other capital revenues tend eventually to be fully collected. In 2017, the amount of accounts receivable that was considered doubtful was 34.5 billion euros, or 59% of current revenues. Yet, from 2015, LGs must provide allowances for doubtful accounts and the problematic amount not covered by such provisions has fallen to about 15.3 billion euros or 26% of current revenues (source: Ministry of the Interior from AIDA PA database, Bureau van Dijk – A Moody's Analytics Company).

At the same time, LGs' off-budget debt increased in the last few years: +54% between 2011 and 2016 (Corte dei Conti, 2016). Off-budget debt is represented by (usually current) expenditures not budgeted for and which must then be compensated for extraordinarily, causing difficulties to balance the budget. For the fiscal year 2016, the Italian Court of Auditors has evaluated off-budget debts at a level of 1.4 billion euros, or 2.6% of current expenditures, involving about one-quarter of all LGs (Corte dei Conti, 2018).

A further way to assess fiscal tensions among LGs would point to the sum of their arrears. Unfortunately, as in most EU countries, there is no reliable data about their exact sum. In 2013, they were officially estimated to be at about 90 billion euros, but some further estimates would have raised this sum to about 100 billion euros (Raffer & Padovani, 2019). Moreover, the Ministry of Economy and Finance organised a large-scale buyback of the local debt causing these arrears (Unicredit, 2016, p. 10) making the picture even fuzzier. Between 2013 and 2015, Italian LGs received 29 billion euros in loans from the central government to clear their overdue payables.

Therefore, the actual vulnerability of Italian LGs before the pandemic is difficult to assess.

Immediate aftermath of COVID-19

ANCI, the national association of municipalities, provided an analysis of the financial vulnerability of Italian municipalities in April 2020 (ANCI, 2020). This analysis is of interest as it implicitly contains three different indicators of vulnerability. First, commitment-based accounting surplus (*avanzo d'amministrazione*) represents the financial buffer that could be used in these emergency situations. Twenty-eight percent of municipalities did not have financial buffers.

Second, the reserve for doubtful accounts is set as another important vulnerability measure. While, on average, this reserve is 5% of current expenditures, municipalities with less than 10,000 inhabitants with a rate below 5% seemed more vulnerable than bigger municipalities, where, for example, such reserve jumps to 10% for municipalities between 60 and 100 thousand inhabitants.

Third, the most important element in ANCI's analysis is the expected reduction in 2020 of 17 typologies of own revenues. ANCI submitted a survey to the more than 100 provincial capital municipal governments in April. Fifty-six percent of them answered and reported an overall decrease in their own revenues of between 9% and 21% (ANCI, 2020). In particular, the following revenues were expected to be hit the hardest:

- Tourism tax (-77%).
- Fees from services relative to culture, tourism and sport (-50%).
- Local police fines (-49%).
- School and kindergarten fees (-39%).
- Occupation of public land tax (-37%).
- Public transportation and parking fees (-35%).

An independent analysis by the University of Bologna and adopted by the National Council for Economics and Labour (CNEL) followed a different method, where the expected reduction of 50+ typologies of own revenues was estimated based on evaluations by municipality officials and ascertained that the decrease in own revenues was expected to be between 13.7% and 22% (CNEL, 2020). According to this analysis, the most vulnerable municipalities would be those with high level of financial autonomy and, in particular, touristic and larger municipalities. The paradox that emerges is that municipalities considered to be more financially vulnerable before COVID-19, that is those more financially dependent from central and regional governments, and with a difficult current balance, were likely to be less affected by this new crisis precisely because their main revenue source, i.e. grants, were unlikely to be cut.

Final remarks

The case of Italian LGs depicts a country case where basically the administrative structure and fiscal rules have not been changed and no extraordinary powers were devolved to municipalities.

The central government enacted special measures mainly leveraging on revenues support: postponing municipal revenue collection deadlines contrasted by cash advances during the lockdown period, then bank overdraft facilities and relief grants after the first lockdown period for a total amount of 19% of current expenditures plus debt instalments. On the expenditure side, the central government and banks agreed to postpone capital instalments of mortgages, which amount only 2.5% of current expenditures plus debt instalments.

The distribution of financial resources could not have gone in the hands of needy municipalities. A sizeable amount of financial resource was distributed as bank overdraft facilities (12 out of 19%), therefore, new debt for municipalities, distributed on the basis of the level of arrears at the end of the 2019 fiscal year. This means that these resources were distributed to those municipalities already in financial distress, while most vulnerable municipalities are those with a high level of financial autonomy, and in particular, touristic and larger municipalities, normally in better financial health. Furthermore, the central government's relief grants (the remaining 7 out of 19%) could have been distributed to municipalities also on the basis of standard needs and, thus, facilitating those municipalities with lower financial autonomy, and again less affected by the pandemic.

Finally, considering that most resources were provided as debt, that the relief grants were considered below the expected revenue losses, and that capital debt instalments were just postponed by one year, it can be asserted that the financial imbalances of municipalities were postponed and further decisions on how to help municipalities coping with their financial vulnerability must be taken at a later time.

8 Portugal

Susana Jorge and Liliana Pimentel

Country profile: Portugal

Population	10.3 million inhabitants (2019)
Government system	Unitary country and republic ruled by a semi-presidential system
Territorial organisation	Two levels: municipalities (*concelhos*) and civil parishes or sub-divisions of municipalities (*freguesias*).
Number of LGs	308 municipalities and 3,091 parishes; there are also 2 autonomous island regions (regional governments), including 30 of the total 308 municipalities (2018).
LG average size	33,524 inhabitants (municipalities); 56% of the population lives in cities of more than 50,000 inhabitants.

Source: OECD/UCLG (2019).

Introduction

According to the 1976 Constitution (lastly amended in 1989), Portugal is a unitary country with a republic ruled by a semi-presidential system. Its legislative power is composed of a unicameral Parliament (*Assembleia da República*) whose members are elected for a four-year term. The Government is led by the Prime Minister and the Head of State is the President of the Republic who is elected for a five-year term. Local democracy was established in the mid-1970s and it has been developing ever since (OECD/UCLG, 2019). Accordingly, although a unitary country, the administrative and democratic organisation of the Portuguese State comprises local governments (LGs) (municipalities, civil parishes, municipalities associations, and other entities), municipalities being the most important.

There are 308 municipalities, currently divided between small (186 up to 20,000 inhabitants), medium (98 between 20,000 and 100,000 inhabitants), and large size (24 above 100,000 inhabitants). Civil

DOI: 10.4324/9781003274278-8

parishes are territorial divisions of municipalities, performing particular competences, as well as other delegated by municipalities. An administrative reform happened in 2013 reduced the number of civil parishes from 4,260 to 3,091.

Since the late 1970s, municipalities are autonomous from the central government, managing local resources aiming at satisfying the needs of local populations. Still, they are subject to administrative tutelage from the central government. Local politicians are directly elected every four years, to the Executive Board (*Câmara Municipal*) and Deliberative Council (*Assembleia Municipal*), which are the representative bodies of the municipality.

Despite being autonomous, due to a centralisation tradition and the financial regime in practice, municipalities are often quite financially dependent on resources coming from central government, making them quite vulnerable, especially the smaller and rural ones, which, besides the limited taxation powers common to all, collect low amounts of local property and business taxes. Considering that about 60% are of small size, most Portuguese municipalities do not have enough revenue of their own to exert their autonomy, so financial dependency is a severe limitation to that (Jorge, 2015). Therefore, to carry on with their activities and investments, most municipalities depend on external resources, including, up to a certain extent, debt, which creates further issues regarding debt management and repayment, increasing vulnerability.

During the financial crisis that led Portugal to sign the "Memorandum of Understanding on Specific Economic Policy Conditionality" with the so-called *Troika* (i.e. European Commission, ECB, and IMF) in May 2011, several legal measures were implemented allowing to re-establish municipalities' financial equilibrium, creating some buffers. From 2014, conditions started to be prepared for a decentralisation process, which formally began in 2018, transferring to municipalities several public services so far provided centrally.

Administrative structure and fiscal rules

Understanding vulnerability before COVID-19

Municipalities have specific attributions established by law in the domains of rural and urban equipment, energy, transport and communications, education (excluding universities and teaching staff), heritage, culture and science, leisure and sport, health (excluding hospitals, doctors, and nurses), social care, housing, civil protection, environment and basic sanitation, consumer protection, promotion of development, local planning and urbanism, municipal police, and external cooperation.

In Portugal, municipalities are autonomous from the central government, managing their own property, finances, and budget. Proper revenue sources are service provision, property management, and local taxes. Municipalities also benefit from a share of public resources coming from the central government via transfers, which is the most important source of revenue for about 60% of them. Also, grants from the European Union are important sources for financing capital expenditure.

In 2007, a reform of the Local Finance Law changed the transfers system, creating the Municipal Social Fund (FSM). It also gave municipalities a share of personal income taxes. In 2013, a new LG reform redefined municipal responsibilities. A revised Local Finance Law, effective in 2014, was enacted with the goal of strengthening fiscal sustainability and increasing transparency and accountability (OECD/UCLG, 2019).

A process of decentralisation of further competences from the central government has been initiated in 2018. Especially, since 2019, a new decentralisation programme has been gradually implemented over three years to revise the former Local Finance Law of 2013. The reform aims to transfer new responsibilities to municipalities in a wide range of domains, with a special focus on education, healthcare, and transport. The intention is to increase the share of public resources spent at the local level and to intensify inter-municipal cooperation, including at metropolitan level.

Municipalities' vulnerability was reduced by austerity and fiscal consolidation measures (namely those imposed by the *Troika*) from 2012 as a consequence of the public finance crisis, with about 80% of municipalities overcoming vulnerability issues by 2019 through financial buffers.

The measures included more effective rules with regard to budgetary balance, debt limits, the creation of municipal early warning and financial recovery mechanisms, and requirement for the annual accounts to be audited. A law to control commitments and arrears was passed in 2012, limiting payment periods for most expenditures to a maximum of 90 days. The Local Finance Law passed in 2013 required municipalities in financial stress to present financial restructuring plans. Also, the State Budget Laws from 2013 and 2014 brought restrictions applied to municipalities regarding debt ceilings and revenue estimations to avoid over-budgeting. Total net debt (including that of municipal-owned companies) cannot exceed 1.5 times the average of the last three years of collected current revenues. Early warning mechanisms for fiscal stress concern reaching and exceeding the debt limit, and a total revenue execution level below 85% of the estimation.

Overall, there was a replacement of short-term debt by long-term debt. In order to meet payment obligations within the time limits, municipalities could apply for financial support programs created by the central government, hence replacing commercial debt by financial debt, long-term loans (financial debt) could be contracted to pay short-term financial debt, and short-term loans were authorised only to support treasury needs and should be amortised in the same year.

Rules were also established requiring more accurate and realistic budget estimations, especially for revenue and budgetary balance. Current revenue remained estimated based on the average of the last two years. Considerable changes happened in estimating capital revenue, including requirements that capital transfers could only be considered once approved; and property sales revenue could not be higher than the arithmetic average of the previous three years.

The Commitments and Arrears Law passed in 2012 controlled budgetary execution and, in particular, public expenditure, a critical element in ensuring compliance with the budgetary targets. Non-compliant municipalities were obliged to ask for central governments support via financial plans to re-establish equilibrium (the above financial supporting programs).

Immediate aftermath of COVID-19

In order to face the COVID-19 pandemic, the central government immediately took the following measures to temporarily relax some limits and deadlines (ANMP, 2020):

* Deadlines for submitting annual municipal accounts were postponed.
* Procedures for granting exemptions and benefits to most vulnerable citizens were streamlined.
* The application of the budgetary balance rule principle of sustainability was suspended.
* An exceptional regime was established allowing for the non-observance of the quantitative limits stipulated in the Municipal Adjustment Program (FAM), to municipalities still under financial re-equilibrium plans.

- Flexibility in the procedures related to public procurement, namely, waiving the prior visa of the Court of Auditors and changing the thresholds for applying prior consultation.
- Flexibility of administrative procedures regarding contracting new loans to cover pandemic-related expenses, namely not requiring authorisation from the Deliberative Council.
- Extension of the implementation period of the law regarding the transfer of new competences to municipalities within the decentralisation process.
- Changing the debt limits, revoking the ceiling on the use of only 20% of the available margin at the beginning of each year.
- Suspension, until 30 June 2020, of the two-year term of use of medium and long-term loans.

Revenue structure

Understanding vulnerability before COVID-19

In the last decade, the amount of own revenue has been, on average, around 36% of total revenues for all municipalities, with a slight increase in the last four years, approaching 40%. In large urban municipalities, the average has been 64%, while in small municipalities, it has been 27%, rising up to 30% in the recent years. Therefore, only less than one-third of the total financial resources available in small-size municipalities are internally generated. In general, financial independence grows with the size of the municipalities (Fernandes et al., 2020).

The revenue structure was expected to change after 2018 with the decentralisation process, as resources were expected to increase with the possibility of receiving 7.5% of the VAT collected in the municipality jurisdiction from restaurants and lodging, and the revision of the formulas for calculating transfers from the central government.

Immediate aftermath of COVID-19

Vulnerability increased with the postponement of the deadlines for collecting municipal taxes, namely the Municipal Property Tax (IMI) and the reduction of prices and fees, particularly related to water supply, sewage treatment, and waste collection.

Three factors contributed to reduce vulnerability (ANMP, 2020):

- Anticipation of the introduction of the budget balance of the previous year, in the accounts for the year 2020;

- Cash advances on transfers from the central government, subsidies, European funding, and financing related to investments already approved; and
- The possibility of contracting new short-term loans, duly substantiated and directly related to urgent expenses associated with fighting the pandemic.

For municipalities still applying the Commitments and Arrears Law, the limitation in the estimation of effective revenue was suspended, making the calculation of the amount of available funds more flexible, hence allowing for more payments within the short-term.

Expenditure structure

Understanding vulnerability before COVID-19

Vulnerability in terms of expenditure depends on types of services and how they are provided. There is not much custom for outsourcing, but some services (e.g. public transportation) are provided by municipal-owned enterprises.

Approximately two-third of total expenditure is a current expenditure, of which about 30% is personnel, considered a rigid expenditure. The remaining important components are current consumables for the provision of fundamental services (26.9% in 2019), which cannot be deferred or unaccomplished and transfers to other entities such as charities and civil parishes (14.1% in 2019), which may be deferred depending on agreements. Capital expenditure is about one-third of the total and may not be rigid, as investments and local projects may be postponed (Fernandes et al., 2020). However, some rigidity exists for projects approved and funded by the EU. If services are provided by other entities such as municipal networks/associations or municipal-owned enterprises, municipalities could avoid incurring any direct costs for providing such services in the short run, but the debt of these entities would count proportionally to the total debt limit of each municipality.

Immediate aftermath of COVID-19

Vulnerability increased by higher expenditure with cleaning public spaces and offices, by local police checks during the blockades, and due to the granting of financial support, social assistance, and foodstuffs to people in serious social, economic, and financial distress.

On the other hand, vulnerability reduced because of (ANMP, 2020):

1 A 12-month moratorium on the amortisation due until the end of 2020, of financial assistance loan contracts.
2 An exceptional regime granted for the conclusion of debt settlement agreements, within the water and sewage sectors, where debts subject to settlement agreements were not required to pay interest on arrears or financial interest.
3 The possibility of budgeting new expenditures with equipment, goods and services associated with fighting the pandemic, to be eligible for financing via the Municipal Social Fund.

Also, costs for providing fundamental and non-fundamental services were reduced, namely during the confinement, when basic public services, such as schools and public transportation, had been suspended, while other activities such as maintaining green and common areas or providing public services for tourists, and so on, were simply cancelled.

Vulnerability outlook

Understanding vulnerability before COVID-19

Vulnerability is difficult to assess, but some issues could be identified. For instance, until 2007, municipal debt was limited to a percentage of investment expenditure, allowing entities to increase their debt levels to unsustainable amounts; also, inflated budgets allowed for uncontrolled expenditure (Padovani et al., 2021). During the crisis that led Portugal to get external financial support from *Troika* in 2011, several laws were passed, imposing fiscal discipline and the capacity to forecast financial vulnerability in the whole of Public Administration.

The effect of these measures aiming at overall financial sustainability started to be felt from 2014. Before the pandemic, the great majority of municipalities were complying with legal requirements. These disciplinary measures allowed municipalities to overcome some vulnerability issues and become more resilient to crises.

Some financial and other statistical data were available before the crisis, such as the Municipalities' Financial Yearbook (Fernandes et al., 2020) prepared by civil society non-official entities and academics, reporting on budgetary and financial condition of Portuguese municipalities, providing a ranking based on a few indicators.

A medium-term financial planning scheme guided municipalities through the crisis with the use of monitoring and risk control tools. Financial planning included monthly questionnaires by the Local Government General Department (within the central government) on pandemic-related expenditure throughout the crisis. There was also a questionnaire by the Municipalities' National Association. Data were not made public at the time of this study.

Immediate aftermath of COVID-19

There was no statistical data available at the time of this study, but it is expected that debt levels will increase, and some capital expenditure will be postponed due to rescheduling of some local projects that lost priority in face of urgent COVID-19-related expenditure. A balance between financial sustainability and COVID-19 emergencies will be difficult to make because, in several municipalities, extra unplanned spending (combined with reduced revenue and increased debt) may jeopardise the continuity of financial balance. Moreover, the delay of some investment projects may also compromise the provision of certain local public services.

Law 50/2018 settled the basis for decentralisation, without adding activities in new domains. This process is still ongoing (it was delayed due to the pandemic) and is likely to accentuate municipalities vulnerability if, in fact, the new competences are not provided with the appropriate resources.

Final remarks

All in all, although difficult to measure at this point, financial vulnerability in Portuguese municipalities, representing the most important level of LGs, has been clearly affected by their financial regime and financing structure.

The COVID-19 pandemic led to yet another package of legislative measures also affecting municipalities, but the administrative structure and financial regime of municipalities were not changed to deal with the pandemic. Main measures applied to these entities during this health and sanitary crisis concerned temporarily with relaxing debt limitations, anticipating cash advances from transfers, and allowing for extra unplanned expenditure, namely concerning the social area.

The central government, realising municipalities' vulnerability, did not enforce previously established budgeting measures and relaxed prior demands and fiscal constraints for the forthcoming one to two years. Also, several administrative controlling procedures were loosened. These were nevertheless temporary measures and do not affect the financial regime already revised in 2018.

Therefore, the main challenge Portuguese municipalities have been facing is to find a balance between maintaining the financial sustainability, so hardly reached in the latter years, and increased spending and reduced own revenue (namely from property and business taxes, and from service provision, e.g., museums, sports facilities, parking). The improved financial condition of most municipalities, reached in the latter years, allows some resistance to the crisis situation but, nevertheless, difficult decisions are likely to be made regarding prioritising new unexpected pandemic-related expenditures at the expense of other local projects, and debt levels are most likely to rise. Large municipalities, which are more financially independent and, therefore, less vulnerable, are likely to be more affected by the pandemic, given the greatest impact on their own revenues.

9 Spain

Isabel Alijarde Brusca

Country profile: Spain

Population	46.9 million inhabitants (2019)
Government system	Unitary state and parliamentary monarchy
Territorial organisation	Three tiers, state level, autonomous communities (*comunidades autónomas*), and local governments
Number of LGs	50 provinces (*provincias*), 8,131 municipalities (*municipios*), four island councils of the Balearic Islands, and seven island councils of the Canary archipelago (2020)
LG average size	5,728 inhabitants; 84% of municipalities have fewer than 5,000 inhabitants

Sources: OECD/UCLG (2019); National Institute of Statistics (2021), Spain https://www.ine.es; Treasury, Spain https://www.hacienda.gob.es.

Introduction

Spain is a parliamentary monarchy defined in the 1978 Constitution. Territorially, it is organised through three levels of government: central state, autonomous communities, and local government (LGs) (provinces and municipalities). In 2020, public expenditure represented 42.1% of GDP. As for the distribution among levels of government, about 35% corresponds to central government, 28% to autonomous communities, and 10.7% to LGs. The other 26.3% corresponds to National Health and Social Service (based on 2018 data).

In LG area in Spain, there are 50 provinces, 8,131 municipalities, and 11 islands. The provinces are determined by the association of municipalities within territorial limits and collaborate in the management of the municipalities that comprise them. In the islands, the island councils are similar to the provinces. The municipality is a public administration based on the territory of the municipal area and there are

DOI: 10.4324/9781003274278-9

great varieties between them in terms of size and economic activity. The largest municipality is M*f*adrid (3,132,463 inhabitants) and the smallest is Illán de Vacas, in Toledo (6 inhabitants). Furthermore, 84% of municipalities have less than 5,000 inhabitants, but only 13% of the population lives in them. The three types of entities have their own legal personality and management autonomy. The municipalities have their own government and administration, where the government is composed of mayors and councillors.

However, the regulation of the municipalities is defined by the central government and the autonomous communities. As for local responsibilities, this depends on the population size of the LGs. There are some mandatory "core competencies" for all the municipalities and other optional tasks. The core competences for compulsory local services include in all municipalities: public lighting, cemetery, waste collection, street cleaning, home supply of drinking water, sewerage, access to population centres, and paving of public roads. In municipalities with a population greater than 5,000 inhabitants, in addition, there are public parks, public libraries, and waste treatment. Municipalities with a population of more than 20,000 inhabitants have to take care also of civil protection, evaluation, and information on situations of social need and immediate attention to people in a situation or at risk of social exclusion, prevention and extinction of fires, and sports facilities for public use. Municipalities with a population of more than 50,000 inhabitants have to deal also with collective urban passenger transport and the urban environment.

Administrative structure and fiscal rules

Understanding vulnerability before COVID-19

The LG is the third level of government in Spain and the closest to the citizens. It is composed of different type of entities: municipalities, provinces, autonomous cities, and the decentralised entities of all the above (organism autonomous, business entities, and not for profit entities). Its main characteristic is that it is regulated by central government, differently from the autonomous communities with more autonomy. This means that the legal framework for LGs is established by the central government.

In 2012, taking into account the reforms of the European Economic Governance six pack that reinforced the Stability and Growth Pact (SGP) of the European Union, the Spanish Government approved the Organic Law on Financial Stability and Financial Sustainability (hereinafter "LOEPSF"). This law established procedures for the effective implementation of the rules of budgetary stability and financial sustainability, reinforcing the commitment of Spain to fiscal sustainability in the EU. The law aims to guarantee the financial sustainability of all public administrations, reinforcing trust, and confidence in the stability of the Spanish economy.

The law requires that all entities of the public sector conform to three fiscal rules:

- Rule of Budgetary Stability or Budgetary Balance. This rule requires that the preparation, approval, and execution of budgets and other actions that affect the expenditure or income of the different entities be made within a framework of budgetary stability, consistent with European regulations. The budgetary stability of the LG is defined as the balance or structural surplus defined in the European System of Accounts-ESA (net lending/borrowing). The rule is applied using consolidated data, including both the main entity and other dependent entities that are classified as non-market producers. For business entities dependent on LG that are considered market producers, budgetary stability is defined as the position of financial equilibrium, determined on the basis of their income statement.
- Expenditure Rule. The law formulates a target for government expenditures, so that computable government expenditure cannot increase above the medium-term GDP growth rate (set by the Ministry of Economy) in accordance with European regulations.
- Rule of Financial Sustainability. The law defines financial sustainability as the ability to finance present and future commitments within the limits of deficit and public debt. In particular, it requires two different requirements:
  - Financial debt limits. The law establishes a debt limit for each level of administration with respect to the Gross Domestic Product: 44% for central administration, 13% for autonomous communities, and 3% for local corporations. In the case of LGs, the requirement of 3% is for all the administrations and there are no indications for each entity, although LG regulations establish a limit for total debt with respect to current revenues, that at the moment it is 110%. Another limitation

operates for entities with negative net current deficit/surplus, which cannot contract new debt.

- Commercial debt limits. The law also establishes the sustainability of commercial debt, requiring that the average period of payment to suppliers does not exceed 30 days from the date of acceptance or verification of the goods or services.

In those cases where an entity does not comply with the rules of budgetary stability, the public debt limit, or the principle of expenditure, the LG has the obligation to elaborate an Economic-Financial Plan that covers the current year and the following year in order to ensure that a positive financial situation is re-established and all requirements are achieved.

Finally, the law prevents the use of budgetary surplus for reducing the level of debt and cash surpluses must be used only for investments that are financially sustainable.

Immediate aftermath of COVID-19

In March 2020, the central government passed several decrees to face the pandemic crisis in Spain. In particular, the Royal Decree-Law 8/2020, issued on 17 March 2020, regarding extraordinary urgent measures to face the economic and social impact of COVID-19 includes some measures for LGs. Those entities that had a budget surplus in 2019 were allowed to increase capital expenditures above the forecast level for the area of social services and social promotion, provided that the entities complied with the fiscal rules stated as compulsory at that moment (that is budgetary stability, expenditure, and financial sustainability). Moreover, LG could use 20% of the budgetary surplus of 2019 to cover extraordinary capital expenditure for social services. Nevertheless, this type of expenditure would not be included to determine the expenditure rule.

Hence, with the development of the pandemic, and due to the serious situation it has caused, the central government has approved the suspension of fiscal rules during the years 2020 and 2021. This decision has been taken after different propositions by the association of LGs that considered it nearly impossible to comply with the fiscal rules during this period due to the high level of expenditures that LGs are experiencing during the pandemic crisis. This was facilitated by the European Commission's decision to "pause" the requirements to member states to meet the fiscal targets.

Revenue structure

Understanding vulnerability before COVID-19

Royal Decree 2/2004 that regulates local administration (article 2) defines the following financial resources available to Spanish LGs for financing local services:

a   Revenues generated by LG's assets and other private resources.
b   Own taxes classified in fees, special contributions and taxes, and the surcharges required on taxes by autonomous communities or other local entities.
c   Participations in taxes levied by the State and the autonomous communities.
d   Transfers received from other entities.
e   Revenues perceived as public prices.
f   Debt and credit operations.
g   The product of fines and sanctions in the scope of their powers.
h   Other public benefits.

The law limits contracting debts exclusively for financing invest-ments and requires the following conditions before increasing debt:

*   The entity must have a current budgetary surplus (current reve-nues less current expenditures in the budgetary statement).
*   The total debt cannot exceed 110% of current revenues.

The report by the Spanish Ministry of Finances (2020, p. 44) shows that for 2017, the revenues from local taxes represented 43.6% of total local revenues, with municipal property tax accounting for 26.8% of total local revenues, while current transfers from other entities, which originated mainly from participations in the taxes of the central and regional governments, were 31.6% of total local revenues. Only 3.25% of local revenues came from financial operations, including financial debt or the sale of financial assets. This shows that LGs rely on local taxes and on central and regional government transfers.

Immediate aftermath of COVID-19

The pandemic has led to important decreases in LG revenues, mainly in local taxes and fees, due to the low level of economic activity. This has affected directly the budgets of municipalities that have had to cover not only forecasted expenditures but also important increases in them due to the pandemic (see hereinafter).

After the suspension of the fiscal rules, LGs with accumulated cash surplus have had the flexibility to use some of these surpluses to cover expenditures caused by the pandemic and not only investments. Furthermore, the association of LGs asked the central government the creation of a Fund for Economic and Social Recovery, directed to all local entities, with special attention to those that do not have cash surpluses or are considered in a situation of financial risk and designated for local recovery actions derived from the COVID-19 pandemic. In 2020, the central government did not take specific actions to support LGs to cover expenditures but through European funding, some grants for public transport and digital innovation were approved. Additionally, some regional governments have approved extraordinary grants for LGs.

Furthermore, those LGs that had not accumulated any or enough cash surpluses have also been trying to balance budgets by turning to financial debt, although the law limits total debt to 110% of current revenues.

Expenditure structure

Understanding vulnerability before COVID-19

The structure of expenditures varies across LGs depending on the size of the municipalities and on the services provided. In any case, current expenditures are always higher than capital expenditures. On average, for the total of municipalities, 88.2% of non-financial expenditures are for current items and the remaining 11.8% are investments (direct investments and transfers to other entities for investments) (Spanish Ministry of Finance, 2020). In particular, personal expenditures cover around 38% of non-financial expenditures and other current goods and services another 38% (Spanish Ministry of Finance, 2020). This means that non-financial expenditures are rather rigid, that is they are expenditures that are difficult to reduce. Expenditures for the debt interest payments represent just 1.5% of the total non-financial expenditures.

With respect to the functional classification of expenditures, LGs have the highest expenditures in the production of public goods of social character, which include health, education, housing, water sanitation, waste collection, culture, and sports. They represent, on average, around 54% of total non-financial expenditures (Spanish

Ministry of Finance, 2020). Social services represent around 11.5% of total non-financial expenditures.

However, there are big differences among entities as the services provided are different also depending on the size of the municipalities. Entities with fewer inhabitants have less responsibilities in providing services and a higher level of government must provide some services.

Immediate aftermath of COVID-19

LGs have faced important increases in expenditures that have not been forecast, such as disinfection programs and the installation of technical means for the adaptation of local buildings to the pandemic necessities, acquisition of protection devices for public workers, compensation for a total or partial suspension of contracts, expenses related to granting aid to guarantee access to all essential supplies (water, gas, electricity, rental of housing, food), expenses related to teleworking measures with the acquisition of equipment or provision of computers, and Internet or communication services. Furthermore, LGs have cooperated in the reactivation of commerce, small and medium-sized companies, and cultural groups, leading to expenses of diverse nature, not foreseen in the budgets of local entities where some rearrangements had to be done.

The central government has allowed that, for the period of the pandemic, LGs that do not have enough credit for these expenditures can approve extraordinary budgets for them, which implies a change to the process of budgetary modifications. In order to facilitate the process for budgetary modifications, the government approved a simple procedure for governments to approve the change of the destination of the resources, so that local councils can approve modifications with a simple majority. Some flexibility has also been introduced in the procurement of services due to the extraordinary necessities to face the pandemic.

Vulnerability outlook

Understanding vulnerability before COVID-19

Since the approval of the LOEPSF in 2012, LGs have reduced the level of debt and a large majority of municipalities have improved their public finances. Most LGs have registered a fiscal surplus since 2012, which contrasts with the deficit registered in the rest of Spanish public administration (Alloza and Burriel, 2019). However, there is great heterogeneity across entities. Due to the restrictions of the Law, since 2012, LGs have reduced capital expenditures and investments as well as the level of debt: Overall, the stock of debt has been reduced by 41% with respect to the maximum level reached in 2012.

One indicator of the financial sustainability of LGs is the ratio of debt to current income, which has been reduced by nearly half since 2012, reaching 36% in 2018 (Alloza and Burriel, 2019). All in all, the LG sector registers an excessive deficit procedure of 2.1% of GDP, a value lower than the debt limit of 3% established by the LOEPSF. This improvement in the situation is due both to the increase in revenues and to the reduction of expenses after the financial crisis of 2008 and due to the rules introduced by the LOEPSF.

This situation has allowed many LGs to achieve budgetary and cash surpluses. In normal times, Spanish law impedes the use of these surpluses for current expenditures, which must be used for the prepayment of debt or for financially sustainable investments.

As a consequence, from an aggregated perspective, the LGs sector presented, in general, a healthy financial situation before the pandemic, compatible with the debt limits established in the LOEPSF, although with a high level of heterogeneity. There was still room for improvement, particularly in the case of medium and large-size municipalities.

Immediate aftermath of COVID-19

The central government has the legal capacity to enact fiscal and financial regulations for LGs. With the pandemic, the central government has been aware of the financial problems caused to LGs, and considering the healthy financial situation and the accumulation of surpluses, since March 2020, they have been allowed to spend the budgetary surpluses accumulated from previous years.

Although there has been a debate and continuous dialogue with the central government in order to use cash surpluses to cover the increase in expenditures due to COVID-19, there was no clear regulation released in 2020. However, it was known that most LGs had cash surpluses that could have been used to finance the modifications of credits and the expenditures derived from the pandemic when the government approved it. At the end of the year, many LGs reached a deficit, which would require some financial support from the central government, but the actions taken were scarce and only some grants to cover the deficits of public transport during the pandemic and for digital innovation have been approved.

Final remarks

Spain reveals a country case where fiscal rules have been temporally suspended due to the implications of the pandemic for local finances, in line with the flexibility introduced by the European Union in the application of the fiscal rules stated by the SGP. This has been an important challenge for LGs that now can decide about expenditures with more flexibility and have to consider diverse public policies to recover from the pandemic. Furthermore, as revenues were enough to cover all the expenditures, they could use debt to finance their activities.

The healthy financial situation of most LGs has allowed them to cover partially the expenditures due to the pandemic, with some rearrangements in their budgets. However, as the central government has the control of local finances, this requires its approval.

The suspension of fiscal rules also introduced flexibility in the use of cash surpluses to finance the modification in the budget appropriations to the different types of expenditures during the crisis.

All in all, many LGs have reached a deficit in the 2020 fiscal year, and municipalities have increased their level of debt, as has already occurred with the 2008 financial crisis. In spite of the positive trends in local finances since 2012, the pandemic has deteriorated LGs finances, evidencing their vulnerability under these extraordinary circumstances with somewhat minimum support from the central government.

10 United States of America

Mary Schulz, Eric Scorsone, and Simone Valle de Souza

Country profile: United States of America

Population	328.2 million inhabitants (2019)
Government system	Federal state and presidential republic
Territorial organisation	Three tiers, states, counties, municipalities/ towns/townships
Number of LGs	3,031 counties, 35,748 municipalities/towns/ townships (2017)
LG average size	9,086 inhabitants; 80% of municipalities have fewer than 5,000 inhabitants

Source: OECD/UCLG (2019).

Introduction

The United States is organised under a federal system in which power is shared by the federal and state governments. A power reserved to the state governments is the creation and management of local governments (LGs). This arrangement results in each of the 50 state governments having its own system of laws detailing the types of LGs and their authorities and limitations. As of 2017, the United States has 38,779 general-purpose governments. Across the states, there are 3,031 counties. Of the 35,748 sub-county (municipal and township) governments, 80% have 5,000 inhabitants or fewer. Sub-county governments with greater than 200,000 inhabitants number 123 or 0.34% of the total.

Administrative structure and fiscal rules

Understanding vulnerability before COVID-19

Balanced budget requirements, bankruptcy procedures, and debt limits are fiscal principles that influence the financial management of LGs. Most states have formal balanced budget requirements. Some

DOI: 10.4324/9781003274278-10

states have explicit balanced budget requirements. In other states, the requirement comes from a constitutional limitation on indebtedness or some other budgetary provision. The political culture of a state reinforces these requirements and it also influences the amount of state resources devoted to state assistance, oversight, and enforcement. For example, Tennessee's LGs with debt outstanding (potentially 95 counties and 342 municipalities) must annually submit a balanced budget for approval to the comptroller of the treasury. Balanced budget requirements and debt issuance limits can be tied together for LGs. In Michigan, to qualify to issue municipal securities, the municipality cannot end the immediately preceding fiscal year with a deficit in any fund, unless the municipality has filed a financial plan to correct that deficit condition that is acceptable to the state treasury department. Additionally, a stated purpose of the primary budget statute for Michigan's LGs is "to prohibit deficit spending by a local unit of government."

Municipal governments can be subject to statutory, charter, and constitutional debt limits and these restrictions vary by state. Limitation structures include percentage of assessed property value, interest rate limits, time restrictions, voter requirements, and state approval (ACIR, 1961). For example, the constitutions of Michigan and Virginia place a debt limitation of 10% of the locality's assessed valuation. Tennessee statutes do not limit LG debt. However, localities with outstanding debt are closely monitored.

Article 1, Section 8 of the U.S. Constitution gives Congress the power to establish uniform bankruptcy laws throughout the United States and Chapter 9 of the U.S. Bankruptcy Code addresses adjustment of debts of a municipality. Only municipalities, not states, can file for Chapter 9. The process for authorising a Chapter 9 municipal filing varies by state. Some states (e.g., California, Alabama) grant their municipalities the right to file for Chapter 9 protection on their own. Other states (e.g., Michigan, Ohio) require that municipalities receive state approval before they file. Georgia is the only state that does not allow its municipalities to file for bankruptcy. Under Chapter 9 bankruptcy, the federal court does not liquidate any assets. The municipality retains its property unless it is part of the debt repayment plan established under Chapter 9. Critics of Chapter 9 point out that the bankruptcy process may decrease municipal debt for a locality, but it may not restore its financial health. Fiscal problems that are structural in nature can and often do continue well after going through Chapter 9 bankruptcy.

Immediate aftermath of COVID-19

When the pandemic fully hit in March of 2020, state governments began taking some actions to assist LGs. Across the country, certain audit deadlines were relaxed such as in Massachusetts and New Mexico where municipalities were given three extra months to file their annual financial audit. There were also delays imposed in terms of tax filing deadlines for households and businesses.

Other changes were that some states stood prepared to provide additional loan funds to cover any potential cash shortfalls. At the same time, the United States Federal Reserve Bank also opened a new municipal liquidity facility line that would allow LGs to borrow for cash flow needs. Overall, there were no major changes to the administrative structure in the United States following the onset of the pandemic.

Revenue structure

Understanding vulnerability before COVID-19

There are 50 state-local revenue systems and the rules governing these systems can differ across states and within states by locality. A state's local revenue structure system is affected by a myriad of influences such as a local unit's size, government type, government-provided services, federal mandates, citizen, and elected officials' preferences toward development and growth and social welfare. States also vary as to the authority granted to their local units to levy or modify the types, sources, and amounts of revenue it receives and whether voter approval is required.

LGs revenue sources are derived from a combination of roughly one-third from intergovernmental transfers (mainly federal and state) and two-thirds from own sources in the form of taxes (primarily property, sales, and income), local option taxes (casino/wagering, severance, tourism, etc.) service charges, fees, and fines. Three quarters (37 states) permit local general sales taxes, which according to the most recent Census Bureau statistics generated 13% of local tax revenues. All 50 states permit local property taxes, yielding 72% of local tax revenues. One-quarter or 13 states permit LGs to levy individual income tax, yielding nearly 5% of local tax revenues.

The role of the federal government in American society is influenced by a myriad of factors including ideological preferences of federal elected officials, executive branch officials and justices of the Supreme Court, and organised interest groups. Federal regulatory standards and compliance mandates affecting public functions of LG, e.g. drinking and wastewater systems and low-income housing, has increasingly shifted from the states and localities to Washington, D.C. With this shift came federal resources. However, over the decades, federal priorities expanded from providing assistance to build public infrastructure, support public education, and economic development efforts to providing healthcare benefits, income support, and housing assistance to individuals. Federal grants to LGs have generally increased over the years. The LGs' share of direct federal support is 9% compared to the states' share of 91%. States pass on a portion of their federal revenues to localities to help support services and infrastructure such as primary and secondary education, public welfare, and roads expenses.

With localities having to rely heavily on their own sourced revenues, there will inevitably be fiscal variance among states. For example, the per capita general revenue from own sources in 2018 for Alabama was $2,538, Connecticut $3,613, Illinois $3,785, Mississippi $2,523, and Michigan $2,382. Within states, fiscal disparities also exist. Some localities have greater taxable resources and/or enjoy lower costs for providing basic public services. In Connecticut, research shows that there are significant fiscal disparities among municipalities, mostly due to the uneven distribution of the property tax base and to a lesser extent cost of service differences across the state. These imbalances persist even after accounting for certain state grants aimed at helping communities that have property tax-exempt entities (e.g., colleges, hospitals, other state-owned property). Property taxes account for nearly 75% of taxes levied by LGs to fund basic services and nearly 50% of total own-source revenues. States differ with respect to their policies aimed at equalising fiscal disparities across their localities due to varying fiscal capacities.

The municipal bond market plays a critical role in providing access to revenue streams for the provision of LG public services, especially for capital infrastructure, e.g., roads, water systems, jails, courthouses, government buildings, schools, hospitals, senior centres, airports, etc. General obligation (GO) bonds are secured by the governmental issuer's "full faith and credit" and, thus, its power to levy taxes. GO bonds typically require voter approval and are subject to total debt limits. Revenue bonds typically are secured by dedicated future revenue streams in the form of taxes, tolls, and other user charges expected to be generated by the infrastructure project being financed.

LGs are responsible for nearly two-thirds of total outstanding debt issued by both state and LGs. In 2018, total LG outstanding debt was $1.9 trillion.

Immediate aftermath of COVID-19

As stated earlier, property taxes remain an important mainstay of local revenues. The pandemic has not substantially caused problems in the aggregate for local property tax revenues in the immediate aftermath. The reporting from the U.S. Census Bureau indicates that for the third quarter of 2020, U.S. property tax revenues were up 5.5% as compared to the third quarter of 2019 (U.S. Census Bureau, 2021). There were concerns that some of the larger taxpayers, especially in the commercial sector, may appeal their property values as the pandemic has caused major declines in rental income especially for business tenants. However, in the immediate aftermath of the pandemic, this remained speculation and there was no clear indication of whether this would in fact happen.

Other major revenues sources would be the local income and sales tax revenues and intergovernmental aid. The initial $2 trillion Federal Coronavirus Aid Relief and Economic Security Act (CARES) passed in the spring of 2020 but did not provide any support for lost revenue at the local level. State governments which provide the bulk, about 80%, of LG intergovernmental aid mostly held firm and did not impose severe reduction as has been typical in past recessions. For local income tax, which was only applicable in certain states and for certain LGs, it was likely that there would have been a drop of 5%–7% in the subsequent months (Auerbach, et al., 2020). For local sales tax revenues, which are also restricted to certain states and certain municipalities, the drop was forecasted to be as high as 8%–10% (Zhao and Weiner, 2015).

Besides direct aid to LGs, other parts of the CARES Act had an indirect impact on LG revenues. The direct payments to individuals and unemployment assistance programs lead to an increase in personal income of $1.14 trillion in the second quarter of 2020. Contrast this to a drop in economic production of nearly 30% in the second quarter of 2020. U.S. LGs are heavily dependent on both their own source local revenues and state government based intergovernmental transfers. This huge increase in income buoyed state and local sales tax revenues alleviating a potential crisis from a revenue drop. The same was true of local income tax revenues. Finally, property tax revenues, the largest source revenue, were also positively impacted by the stimulus which helped generate increases in home prices in 2020 reported as 10% growth in

2020 (Case Shiller Index, 2021). A second stimulus bill of $900 billion was passed by the U.S. government. This bill largely continued many of the policies from the first relief bill but in many cases of smaller amounts. This second stimulus bill contained no LG provisions.

Expenditure structure

Understanding vulnerability before COVID-19

The expenditure structure of LGs reflects the basket of services provided by each locality, state and federal mandates, (e.g., environmental protection, public safety, public education), and in some circumstances court judgments.

County and municipality responsibilities vary by locality and can include building and maintaining infrastructure such as roads, bridges, subways, airports; transit services (bus, subway systems) school buildings, hospitals, jails, drinking water, sewer, stormwater systems; solid waste management; utilities; health services; criminal justice, public safety, and first responders; parks, recreation, and culture; housing services; property assessing, tax collection; social services; elections administration; record keeping; libraries; education; and local economic development, and more.

The following financial information on LG expenses is for 2018 and represents all 50 states and the District of Columbia. LG total expenditures were nearly $2 trillion. Education was by far the largest source of LG expenditures at $747 billion (37%). Public welfare, health, hospitals constituted 12%; utilities 11%; police and fire 10%; parks and recreation, housing, sewerage, solid waste 9%; general administration 8%; highways and airports 5%; other 5%; and insurance trust 3%.

The work of LGs is labour intensive. Salaries and wages account for 36% of total LG expenditures (U.S. Census Bureau, 2021). Adding in employee health and retirement benefits would increase labour's share of total expenses well above 50%.

Total outstanding debt held by LGs was nearly $2 trillion, of which long-term debt accounted for 99%. LGs are generally not allowed or tend not to hold much short-term debt. Interest paid on general debt paid $65.4 billion.

Immediate aftermath of COVID-19

The CARES Act did provide funding for LGs to respond to the pandemic. The Coronavirus Relief Fund targeted $150 billion to state and LGs to respond to the pandemic in terms of personal protection equipment, coronavirus testing, new facility management cleaning protocols, hazard pay for frontline workers, expanded food assistance and rental aid for low-income households, and other such spending measures. Larger city and county governments received direct aid from the federal government and smaller governments received aid through their state governments. These measures not only impacted individuals and businesses but also LGs. In general, the money could be used for necessary public health emergency measures that had not been budgeted for and had to be incurred between 1 March 2020, and 31 December 2021. The money could not be used for negative economic impacts or lost revenue issues.

Even with the CARES Act support, the pandemic public health crisis and recession has hit state and LG quite large and much of this would have occurred at the local level and has increased needed expenditures. It is estimated that LGs represent 5% of all U.S. employment or about 6.6 million jobs (BLS, 2021). Since March of 2020, this sector has lost 300 thousand jobs. It is unclear at this time of the exact nature of job losses, but they could be accounted for in areas such as parks and recreation, cultural services and mass transit as social distancing and shut down measures were required.

Vulnerability outlook

Understanding vulnerability Before Covid-19

U.S. LGs generally budget based on a year cycle with some larger governments doing a three or five year cycle with projections (Levine et. al, 2012). This fairly short budget cycle for many LGs does potentially leave them vulnerable to a crisis breaking out or understanding the need to determine long term challenges. That said, the nature of a once in a hundred-year pandemic caught many LGs unaware and off-guard. U.S. local fiscal health is generally measured with a series of indicators related to operating deficits, fund balance reserves, debt and unfunded liabilities related to pension and health care expenses (Levine, 2012).

The best available measures of short term local fiscal health and financial vulnerability are generally related to reserves. Prior to the pandemic, LGs in the United States had built up substantial reserves. There is limited data available on this issue, but recent reporting indicated that from a sample of LGs many help at least 50% in reserves as compared to their overall revenue base (Joffe, 2020). This is well above the traditionally recommended 15%–20% of reserves (Levine et al. 2012). There had also been no reported municipal bankruptcies in several years. Overall, local U.S. fiscal health seemed to be stable and resilient learning up to the Coronavirus pandemic.

Immediate aftermath of COVID-19

Some information was collected soon after the pandemic rises to assess the impact of the pandemic on LGs. The National League of Cities did a survey of 900 municipalities in the fall of 2020 and had the following findings (National League of Cities, 2020). Seventy-one percent of respondents felt that their financial condition would worsen without additional stimulus help from the federal government. Additionally, 30% of respondents said that they had received no CARES Act funding and that many of those that did receive funding said it was inadequate to recover costs imposed by the pandemic. The survey also found that over 90% of respondents had experienced both a spending increase (17% increase on average) and revenue decline (on average 20%) from the pandemic. Therefore, we can see some initial evidence that while LGs may have had strong balance sheets going into the pandemic that conditions were rapidly worsening.

Final remarks

The Coronavirus pandemic has had unprecedented impacts on LG in the United States. Unlike previous economic shocks, this crisis caused both a decline in revenue and an increase in spending. U.S. LGs are front-line providers of critical public services during a public health crisis including medical care, fire and police protection, and drinking water. These services were needed by the public and became more expensive to provide at the same time.

LG did go into this crisis with strong balance sheets and resilience measures in place. However, the scale of the public health and economic crisis has caught many unprepared. New federal measures are critical to maintaining LG services and reducing potential vulnerability to economic and financial pressures.

11 Conclusions

Emanuele Padovani, Simone Valle de Souza, and Silvia Iacuzzi

Comparing financial vulnerability across eight countries

Analysing financial vulnerability across eight countries before the COVID-19 pandemic and in its immediate aftermath has allowed us to reveal differences, but also some common trends. This chapter first summarises findings from the previous chapters in a comparative fashion to make such elements emerge for each field of enquiry and then considers the characteristics which shape local government (LG) financial vulnerability at a global level. Similar patterns of financial vulnerability were identified across different nations to the role of contextual economic, institutional, and organisational circumstances affecting financial vulnerability and the effectiveness of resilience measures. These findings allow also us to review and refine the conceptual framework, highlighting advantages and limitations of a universalistic approach in the analysis of responses to transboundary crises. Notably, they reveal that a higher financial vulnerability in LGs in the next years could be expected without further interventions.

The chapter concludes with remarks on future research that may be needed to sharpen models used to monitor financial vulnerability, to understand how the COVID-19 pandemic has impacted LGs, to identify gaps in central governments' relief policy, and the potential long-term changes that may be observed amongst LGs.

Field #1. Administrative structure and fiscal rules

LGs are the lowest tier of government, the ones closest to citizens. They are not always recognised by the constitution, as in the case of Australia and the United States, but they are generally subject to state or regional laws and rules regarding the administrative structures that characterise them and in some cases the activities they perform. For example, in Italy, revenue and expenditure autonomy is recognised by the constitution, while in Germany, local fiscal autonomy as a constitutional element is

DOI: 10.4324/9781003274278-11

limited by state law. Regulations can also restrict revenues by capping local rates and fee charges. For example, in Australia, LGs are subject to annual property tax limitations that impose ceilings on their increase.

Before COVID-19

In general, before the pandemic LGs were subject to basic rules related to the need to balance budgets, limiting borrowing capacity, and bankruptcy provisions, which helped keep under control their financial vulnerability.

The European System of Accounts (ESA) which applies to EU countries (Austria, Germany, Italy, Portugal, and Spain in our analysis) prescribes that budgets must be balanced. A similar regulation applied to LGs in Bosnia and Herzegovina, the US, and Australia.

Also, before the pandemic, the borrowing capacity of LGs was generally subject to approval or regulations and the amount of debt that could be taken on by a LG was limited. In Austria, debt ceilings were part of the Austrian Stability Pact, which specifies targets for budget deficit, the level of debt, expenditure growth, etc. Australian LGs were not subject to debt ceilings, but they were required to report debt servicing and liquidity ratios at recommended levels, 20% and 1.5%, respectively, and borrowings could only be raised to finance the acquisition of assets. Bosnian regulations limited total exposure under guarantees issued to 30% of the amount of operating revenues generated in the previous fiscal year, established a ceiling of 5% of operating revenues generated in the previous fiscal year for short-term borrowing and conditioned long-term indebtedness to annual repayments not exceeding 18% of the operating revenues generated in the previous fiscal year. In Spain, the Rule of Financial Sustainability set financial debt limits at 3% of the GDP, prescribed that commercial debt limits did not exceed 30 days from acceptance and verification of goods and services, and limited debt at 110% of current revenue. In the case of Germany, long-term debt was restricted to fund capital spending while short-term credits were restricted to ensure liquidity needs. Debt ceilings were also defined in Italy. All in all, in Australia, Bosnia and Herzegovina, Germany, borrowing needed to be approved by external agencies or central government ministries before the pandemic, while in Austria, Italy, Portugal, Spain, and the United States specific debt ceilings were fixed by state, regional, or national rules.

Bankruptcy provisions differed between the different LG systems. In certain areas of Australia, bankrupt councils were placed under administration and were obliged to make ongoing changes to expenditure and income to become viable. Italy had a bankruptcy procedure in place, which was similar to debt clearance plans for private entities. In Bosnia, the bankruptcy law prevented bankruptcy proceedings against LG and allowed them only against their subsidiaries. Austria, Germany, Portugal, and Spain did not have bankruptcy provisions for LGs.

Immediate aftermath of COVID-19

As far as the maintenance or relaxation of LG rules and structures, the eight countries under investigation can be divided into two groups with respect to their immediate reaction to COVID-19.

The first group includes those countries such as Italy, Australia, Bosnia and Herzegovina, and the United States where no extraordinary powers were granted to LGs or minimal temporary changes, such as the postponement of budget approval or auditing filing deadlines, were implemented. For example, in the United States, some small changes were allowed for delays in audit filings, certain tax deadlines were delayed, and some cash flow borrowing measures at state and federal levels were introduced if needed but were sparsely used. With little if any change, rules and structures did not induce financial vulnerability to change significantly with respect to before the pandemic.

The second group includes those countries where more consistent measures have been applied. For example, in Germany, short-term "band-aid" solutions included the suspension of balanced budget requirements for the upcoming year, the suspension of the spending freeze rule in face of revenue shortfalls or imminent deficit, along with a range of measures such as tax reimbursements, support for welfare spending, additional grants for sectors like healthcare or public transport. In Austria, the fiscal rules under the stability pact were suspended. In Portugal, the deadlines for submitting annual municipal accounts were postponed, the application of the budgetary balance rule was suspended, and an exceptional regime to the non-observance of the quantitative limits was stipulated for LGs under financial re-equilibrium plans. Moreover, procedures related to public procurement were eased for Portuguese municipalities, along with changes in the debt limits, revoking the ceiling on the use of only 20% of the available margin at the beginning of each year. In Spain, the central government suspended fiscal rules for two years and Spanish authorities allowed LGs which had surpluses in 2019 to increase capital expenditures in social services providing that they would comply with fiscal rules. In these countries, that is Germany, Austria, Portugal, and Spain, the relaxation of fiscal rules helped ease financial vulnerability in the immediate aftermath of COVID-19, but it may cause financial vulnerability to increase in the future if these measures become structural.

Field #2. Revenue structure

Local revenues depend on transfers from other levels of government, the level of autonomy in raising own taxes and fees, and the services offered to the community. Hence, financial vulnerability often depends on what is known as the level of LG independence.

Before COVID-19

The rate of financial autonomy, such as the share of own revenues in relation to total revenues, differs extensively among LGs across the eight countries under investigation. Before the pandemic, the main sources of local own revenues in most countries could be property tax, personal income, fees and charges for services, or business tax. Own revenues dominated local budgets in Australia, the United States, and Italy; in Austria and Germany, the share of transfers from higher levels of government and own-source revenues was about equal; while in Bosnia and Herzegovina, Spain and Portugal transfers were dominant. A common feature in all countries was that richer municipalities usually larger cities had a higher share of their own revenues to total revenues than poorer municipalities, that is often smaller villages in rural areas. For example, in Portugal, large urban LGs earned about 64% of current revenues from own resources, while this amount shrinks to 27% in smaller ones.

In countries where non-own revenues dominate, municipalities could not influence the level of tax rates, which increased their vulnerability. For example, Germany and Bosnia and Herzegovina received shares of some taxes, such as VAT, for which rates and rules are set at the central level. On the other hand, in Italy and Bosnia and Herzegovina, the central government prescribed the maximum or minimum amount of certain tax rates for municipalities' own revenues, while in Germany, there were no such limitations. In Austria, a complex system of re-distribution of shared revenues across all levels of government was regulated and negotiated every four to six years across the three levels of administration.

Unlike local taxes or shared revenues, transfers from higher levels of government are always an uncertain source of revenue, especially in times of crisis when the budgets of all levels of government are affected. Portugal stands out with more than 60% of local revenues covered by transfers from higher levels of government, Germany is second with about a half of total revenues, followed by Spain 32%, Italy 29%, Bosnia and Herzegovina 14%, Austria 10%, while LGs in the United States and Australia experienced even lower shares of transfers and the least financial vulnerability caused by national policies, since they were directly responsible for the majority of their revenues and were less dependent on state transfers.

Immediate aftermath of COVID-19

To minimise financial pressures to citizens and businesses following the restrictions caused by the pandemic, central governments in Italy, Bosnia and Herzegovina, Australia, and Portugal imposed to postpone, waive, or reduce the collection of local taxes and revenues. Such measures led to a reduction in municipal revenues, the impact of which primarily depends on their share with respect to total local revenues.

On the other hand, central and, in Austria, even regional governments helped LGs with cash advances (Italy, Portugal, Spain), support for some LG centres (Australia), financing capital projects (Australia, Germany), increased low-cost loans from state treasury (Australia), refund of losses in certain tax revenues (Austria, Germany and Italy), stimuli packages for all local entities (Spain), or just some of them (Bosnia and Herzegovina). In the immediate aftermath of COVID-19 emergency raise, there was no additional aid from central governments to LGs only in the United States.

Field #3. Expenditure structure

Looking at expenditures, financial vulnerability is affected by their rigidity and stickiness, that is, they are not flexible enough to adapt to falling revenues, service reduction, and crisis situations in general.

Before COVID-19

The level of rigidity and stickiness is difficult to ascertain nor there is a common understanding about what a rigid or sticky expenditure is. In all contexts, personnel are considered rigid expenses, in a few contexts, that is Italy, Bosnia, and the United States, debt instalments are also part of the rigidity concept. For example, before the pandemic in Bosnia and Herzegovina, there were significant investments and expenditures for upgrading public utility infrastructures and this increased the level of debt and, as consequence, debt instalments. Also, expenditures can be considered rigid or sticky when services must be provided by law or are considered fundamental services and cannot be cut under a minimum level. For this reason, rigidity reached maximum levels in Austria, Bosnia and Herzegovina, Germany, and Portugal. Basic services represented the whole local expenditures in Bosnia and Herzegovina; in Germany, LGs are in charge of a wide range of welfare services that had to be provided under state law even during a crisis and despite differences between economically weak cities, whose budgets were more rigid because of high welfare expenditure, and wealthier areas where they were less rigid. In the last two decades, municipalities in Austria have rapidly increased their level of utility, welfare, and education services. Rigidity is set at levels around 50% in Spain and the United States. However, in the United States, pension expenses were also rigid and should, thus, be added on top of personnel costs. Italy and Australia had, to a certain extent, a lesser level of rigidity. Furthermore, they were also characterised by differences across entities, as in certain LGs, rigidity was as low as 10% in Italy and 27% in Australia.

Immediate aftermath of COVID-19

In all eight countries, expenditures increased in the immediate aftermath of COVID-19 because of pandemic-related issues such as sanitisation, health protection devices for personnel and community, and remodulating social servicing to guarantee social distancing. Only in Austria, Australia, Bosnia, Italy, and Spain, specific stimulus packages were adopted for local communities. In Austria, the federal government started an investment program to guarantee that necessary investments in infrastructure could continue being carried out in 2020 and 2021. In Italy, some LGs waived the payment of local taxes and fees for businesses public services, mainly waste collection and disposal. In Australia, these stimulus packages particularly meant stronger campaigns for supporting regional trade and local food businesses. In Bosnia and Herzegovina, LGs provided a quite large span of measures: distribution of free agricultural packages as support for spring sowing, creation of conditions for more favourable lending, funds for artisans who were greatly affected by the crisis, and grant funds for industrial protection. Spain funded measures not usually foreseen in the budget of a LG with specific packages related to the reactivation of commerce, small and medium-sized companies, and cultural organisations.

To a certain extent, it can be said that there were two different approaches: a "reactionary" approach by those countries (Germany, Portugal, United States) where LGs simply reacted to the events and limited their intervention to an adjustment of their services to the new environmental condition; a "forward-thinking" approach by those countries (Austria, Australia, Bosnia, Italy, and Spain) where LGs enacted stimulus packages for local communities, going beyond their regular role at the expense of becoming more financially vulnerable.

Only in Italy and Portugal, LGs experienced an overall reduction in expenditures. This may depend on the severity and length of lockdowns during the first wave of the pandemic. In certain countries, like Australia, there has been an explicit avoidance of expenditure reduction or slowdown with the aim to support local communities, in line with their "forward-thinking" approach. Only in Italy, Germany, and Portugal, state or federal governments helped LGs by allowing postponing some expenditures, such as debt instalments. The Italian government agreed with the banking system to provide LGs with a one-year moratorium. Portugal saw a similar provision and also allowed LGs not to pay for interests on arrears on debts which were part of settlement agreements for water and sewerage provisions. In Germany, some states adopted minor and temporary regulations to maintain governments liquid, such as spending freeze and cutback measures.

All in all, three groups of countries can be singled out according to the impact of the pandemic and related policies on expenditures in the immediate aftermath of COVID-19. A first group, which includes Austria, Australia, Bosnia, and Spain where LGs not only have experienced an increase in expenditures directly linked to pandemic but that have also enacted a "forward-thinking" approach to support local communities, which has further increased their expenditure. In these countries, no significant reduction of expenditures was reported and, thus, they can be considered those which have increased their financial vulnerability most. A second group of countries is represented by Italy and the United States. The latter has experienced a "reactionary" approach, therefore, LGs have limited their expenditure increase to adjust their services to pandemic, together with no specific financial vulnerability containment provision on the expenditure side. Italy has been "forward-thinking" but its LGs enjoy of a specific provision to reduce expenditures (instalment moratory). The LGs of this second group experienced an intermediate increase of financial vulnerability. In the third group, which has enjoyed the least financial vulnerability increase, German and Portuguese LGs have experienced a "reactionary" approach with no stimulus packages and have enjoyed specific provisions to temporary reduce expenditures.

Field #4. *Assessment of vulnerability*

Measuring and forecasting financial vulnerability can help establish an outlook and, hence, be readier at times of crisis, so as to decrease the impact on financial conditions.

Before COVID-19

Financial forecasts for LG financial vulnerability were approached in different ways. In Bosnia and Herzegovina, Italy, and Portugal, a historic perspective was used with past data helping predict future vulnerability. In Australia, periodic reviews of LGs were undertaken to anticipate critical issues with financial vulnerability and sustainability. In the United States, following the financial crisis of 2007/8, LGs had implemented new financial management practices that took into account risk management and resilience and made financial forecasts less critical. The most advanced assessment of vulnerability was made in Austria, where a prognosis of municipal finances for the next four years was regularly published on an annual basis. In Germany and Spain, financial forecasts were not deemed necessary. No country used stress test techniques to measure financial vulnerability.

Only Australia, Bosnia and Herzegovina, Italy, and the United States used financial indicators to measure performance where and when necessary, which made them somewhat less vulnerable.

The lack of any forecast and measure of LG financial vulnerability made Germany, Portugal, and Spain more financially vulnerable in terms of outlook, while Austrian LGs were more aware and least financially vulnerable from this point of view because of the detailed annual assessment of their financial conditions for the next four years.

Immediate aftermath of COVID-19

Few countries promptly assessed the impact of COVID-19 on local finances: only Austria, Germany, and Italy undertook specific analyses of local revenues and expenditures, with several updated analyses adapted according to developments such as aid programs or lockdowns. Conversely, no formal assessment was undertaken immediately after the appearance of COVID-19 in Australia, Bosnia, and Herzegovina, Portugal, Spain, and the United States. Therefore, the risk of financial vulnerability increased in these countries in the immediate aftermath of the pandemic, while Austria, Italy, and Germany made impact forecasts available to lessen the potential increase of financial vulnerability.

Comparative overview

A comparative overview of the financial vulnerability assessment in qualitative terms for the eight countries analysed is provided in Table 11.1. Across the rows, the different fields of financial

Table 11.1 Comparing the financial vulnerability in the eight countries analysed

Field of financial vulnerability	Timeline	Austria	Australia	Bosnia and Herzegovina	Germany	Italy	Portugal	Spain	USA
1. Administrative Structure And Fiscal Rules	Before COVID-19	△△	△	△△△	△△	△	△△	△△	△
	Immediate aftermath	▲a	▲	▲▲▲	▲a	▲	▲a	▲a	▲
2. Revenue Structure	Before COVID-19	△△	△	△△△	△△	△△	△△△	△△△	△
	Immediate aftermath	▲▲a	▲a	▲▲a	▲a	▲a	▲▲▲a	▲▲a	▲
3. Expenditure Structure	Before COVID-19	△△△	△	△△△	△△△	△	△△△	△△	△△
	Immediate aftermath	▲▲▲	▲▲▲	▲▲▲	▲	▲▲	▲	▲▲▲	▲▲
4. Assessment Of Vulnerability	Before COVID-19	△△△	△△	△△	△△△	△△	△△	△△	△△
	Immediate aftermath	▲	▲▲▲	▲▲▲	▲	▲	▲▲▲	▲▲▲	▲▲▲
Variation Of Overall Level Of Financial Vulnerability		M/H→M	L/M→M/H	H→H	H→L	L/M→L/M-	H→M	H→M/H	L/M→M

Keys: Level of financial vulnerability: △/▲ low; △△/▲▲ intermediate; △△△/▲▲▲ high; before/in the immediate aftermath of COVID-19. L = low; M = medium; H = high

Notes

a Financial vulnerability level is likely to increase should changes remain structural vulnerability have been assessed both before and in the immediate aftermath of COVID-19. The last row provides an overall assessment of how the level of financial vulnerability changed in each country.

Relevant characteristics in shaping local government financial vulnerability

The comparative exercise carried out through the glasses of the framework presented in Chapter 2 allows us not only to comparatively assess the level of financial vulnerability and how it has changed across countries, but also understanding which are the specific patterns of vulnerability in each country and try to understand whether there are some possible cause-effect relationships in consideration of specific national characteristics.

One national characteristic of municipalities that may have had a prominent role in the pressure and magnitude of LGs in reaction to the pandemic is the provision of municipal self-government by the national Constitution. In most of the countries analysed, municipalities are embedded in the Constitution and they are provided with a certain level of decision and financial autonomy. In Australia, the Federation of Bosnia and Herzegovina (FBIH) within Bosnia and Herzegovina and the United States, other "local" governments, such as the states in Australia or the United States or the cantons in FBHI, are granted self-government power, indicating a somewhat higher level of institutional responsibility with respect to local communities. In these cases, municipalities can be considered as having a lesser role than in those countries where they have a constitutional responsibility towards citizens.

Another characteristic that may have had a role in the answer to the pandemic by LGs is the range of services provided. The COFOG international classification, i.e. the Classification of the Functions of Government that classifies government expenditure according to the purpose for which funds are used, provides a rough information about the services covered by LGs. Municipalities in Germany, Portugal, Spain, and the Republic of Srpska (Bosnia and Herzegovina), cover all possible local functions, while at the other end of the spectrum, Australian municipalities provide neither public order and safety, nor health and education services. Being involved in a lesser number of functions may have had a lesser impact on municipalities compared to those nations where they have more responsibilities. This is not only in consideration of the impacts within each function, but also considering the interplays across functions.

More specifically, municipalities may be involved in several different types of services within those functions that have been particularly impacted by the pandemic, namely economic affairs and social protection. For example, Portuguese municipalities have been intensely impacted as they manage services for tourism, economic development, consumer protection, external cooperation, and social program. While American municipalities had a somewhat limited impact as they were just involved with economic development with a very limited responsibilities on social protection.

For all the above-mentioned reasons, the countries analysed may be categorised according to three different profiles depending on the expected role of LGs in managing the effects of the pandemic: low (Australia, Federation of Bosnia and Herzegovina, and the United States), medium (Austria, Republic of Srpska of Bosnia and Herzegovina, and Italy), and high (Germany, Portugal and Spain). These different levels may have had an impact on the magnitude of the effects of the pandemic on local expenditures due to the increase in the demand for services and public intervention.

Finally, municipalities are embedded within a national administrative culture. Two ideal models compete at the international level: On the one hand, the Rechtsstaat model, where the compliance to law and regulations drives public intervention and the State has a prominent role in society; on the other hand, the Public Interest model, where the goal is to provide solutions in the public interest moderating the different needs at stake. According to Pollitt and Bouckaert (2017), Rechtsstaat systems require relative changes in laws and regulations to face factual changes, therefore Rechtsstaat countries such as Austria, Bosnia and Herzegovina, Germany, Italy, Portugal, and Spain should have provided more regulations to help their municipalities to react to the pandemic.

Table 11.2 provides a summary of the relevant national characteristics and the change in financial vulnerability caused by the pandemic in the eight countries analysed. All in all, the analysis shows that municipal financial vulnerability decreased in those countries where it was high or medium-to-high before the pandemic, namely Austria, Germany, Portugal, and Spain. Bosnia and Herzegovina represents the only exception where high financial vulnerability remained high in the immediate aftermath. Austria, Germany, Portugal, and Spain are also countries where LGs are expected to have a high (Germany, Portugal, and Spain) or medium (Austria) active role in managing the impacts of the pandemic. The patterns of the dynamics of financial vulnerability suggest that in these four countries, the central state has

Table 11.2 Relevant national characteristics and financial vulnerability impacts of the pandemic

	Austria	Australia	Bosnia and Herzegovina	Germany	Italy	Portugal	Spain	USA
Municipalities' self-government enshrined by Constitution[a]	Yes	No	RS: Yes FB&H: No	Yes	Yes	Yes	Yes	No
Functions of Government (COFOG) covered by municipalities (max=9)[a], of which:	8	6	RS: 9 FB&H: 8	9	8	9	9	7
• **Responsibilities related to economic affairs**[a]	(none)	(none)	Trade, tourism, employment	Economic development, tourism	Economic development	Tourism, economic development, consumer protection, external cooperation	Tourism, markets	Economic development
• **Responsibilities related to social protection**[a]	Basic social welfare	Child care, elderly care	Centre for social work	Social aid, youth child care	Social services and community assistance	Municipal social program	Social services, allowances, promotion of social reintegration	(none)
Expected Role Of Municipalities In Managing The Pandemic Impacts[b]	M	L	M (RS) L (FB&H)	H	M	H	H	L
Country's Administrative Culture[c]	Rechtsstaat	Public interest	Rechtsstaat	Rechtsstaat	Rechtsstaat	Rechtsstaat	Rechtsstaat	Public interest
Variation Of Overall Level Of Financial Vulnerability[d]	M/H→M	L/M→M/H	H→H	H→L	L/M→L/M-	H→M	H→M/H	L/M→M

Key: L = low; M = medium; H = high

Notes

[a] OECD/UCLG (2019)

[b] Own elaboration from first four characteristics

[c] Pollitt and Bouckaert (2017) except own elaborations for Austria, Bosnia and Herzegovina, Spain, and Portugal

[d] From Table 11.1

provided municipalities with extended extraordinary powers, such as the suspension of balanced budget requirements, fiscal consolidation rules, spending freeze, along with a range of measures as tax reimbursement, support in welfare spending, additional grants. In other words, financial vulnerability related to the fields "1. Administrative structure and fiscal rules" and "2. Revenue structure" has decreased, thanks to wide interventions by the state. To a certain extent, it seems that the central state recognised the active role of municipalities in handling the pandemic actively and pervasively intervened to safeguard their level of financial vulnerability. On the contrary, state interventions were limited to the revenue side (cash advances, grants, etc.) in those countries where municipal financial vulnerability was lower, independently from the municipality expected role in managing the pandemic.

The other fields of financial vulnerability seem not to be linked to the relevant national characteristics. "Forward-thinking" countries, i.e. those whose municipalities reacted with stimulus packages for the local communities (Austria, Australia, Bosnia and Herzegovina, Italy, and Spain), therefore, increasing their level of financial vulnerability (third field of analysis), seem not to follow an ideal pattern, since their municipalities are not expected to play an important role in managing the impacts of the pandemic. This may be due to the limited time horizon of our analysis, which considers just the immediate aftermath of the pandemic, and the lack of measurement of the magnitude of these measures with respect to total expenditures.

Finally, a prompt assessment of the effects of the pandemic on local finances was provided in just three countries, Austria, Germany and Italy, contributing to reducing the level of financial vulnerability attributable to the perception of vulnerability (fourth field of analysis). While this might be explained by the initial high financial vulnerability and the expected medium/high role municipalities were expected to play in facing the crisis, it is hard to appreciate why in Portugal and Spain, which have similar characteristics, this assessment was not carried out.

Final considerations

At the end of this investigation into the effects of the COVID-19 pandemic on the financial vulnerability of LGs across eight countries, a few questions emerge. Which tangible signs will survive the pandemic with respect to the fields of enquiry of financial vulnerability? Will regulatory or managerial measures be able to deal with financial vulnerability in the next years? Will LG systems simply revert to the pre-pandemic period or will they change according to a "new normal?" Will countries with high financial vulnerability (e.g. Australia, Bosnia and Herzegovina, and Spain) gradually revert into medium or even low financial vulnerability? Using what lever, namely releasing administrative/fiscal rules, increasing the possibility to raise revenues, reducing expenditures, or improving the capacity of assessment of vulnerability? Will countries with lower financial vulnerability (e.g. Austria, Germany, Italy, Portugal, and United States) drift gradually to higher level of financial vulnerability, and how? Financial vulnerability is a lively matter and vulnerable in itself: Further investigation may reveal which factors affect most its magnitude in the long run.

Second, financial vulnerability and political attention it attracts are inherently influenced by the policy decisions enacted at the central level in each country. In Australia, the decrease in GDP in 2020 was so mild (–2.4%, compared to –4.8% in OECD countries, –6.7% in the Euro area, and –3.5% in the United States; OECD, 2021) that financial issues were not as crucial. On the contrary, in other countries, the situation was so dramatic in the periods following the "immediate aftermath" that governments enacted huge stimulus packages. In Europe, the "Next generation EU" are forward looking funds which aim at new equilibria in line with the UN 2030 SDGs. In the United States, President Biden urged to "build back better." All in all, the evidence from the eight countries shows that the pandemic often brought to light issues which needed to be addressed and had often been postponed. The pandemic can, thus, be an opportunity to address such issues that will also, directly or indirectly, affect LG financial vulnerability, both in the short run and in the long run. In fact, while further public investments funded by central government may not interfere with LGs' financial vulnerability in the short run, they may increase current expenditures in the long run due to maintenance cost and, in general, operating costs. On the other hand, certain infrastructures may also generate sufficient revenues to cover operating expenditures (e.g. high-speed internet infrastructures) or be financially self-sustainable, thanks to cost reductions (e.g. green energy facilities), but others may be mainly cost generating and at least a portion of them might be socialised (e.g. mass transit systems financed mainly by taxpayers). Further investigation should, thus, shed light on the links between national economic stimuli packages, intergovernmental schemes, and LGs' financial vulnerability.

Finally, there may be a change in the geography of financial vulnerability, as smaller and poorer municipalities with less financial autonomy, which were previously more vulnerable, have been impacted less by the COVID-19 crisis in the short run. On the other hand, larger and richer municipalities, traditionally more autonomous, are now facing higher financial vulnerability (OECD, 2020a). Will the changes introduced by the pandemic be reversed to the pre-pandemic situation? For example, there is a growing debate about the structural changes that metropolitan cities will experience in the future (OECD, 2020b). Will central/federal governments fully rethink the intergovernmental relationships between them and LGs? Or will they leave LGs to their destiny and capability (or not) to change autonomously according to the new settings.

Bibliography

ACIR- Advisory Commission on Intergovernmental Relations (1961). State constitutional and statutory restrictions on local government debt.

Agency for Statistics of Bosnia and Herzegovina (2021). *Agencija za statistiku Bosne i Hercegovine*. Available at: https://bhas.gov.ba/ (Accessed: 1 September 2021).

Ahrens, T., Ferry, L. (2020), 'Financial resilience of English local government in the aftermath of Covid-19', *Journal of Public Budgeting, Accounting & Financial Management*, 32(5), pp. 813–823.

Alloza, M., Burriel, P. (2019). La mejora de la situación de las finanzas públicas de las corporaciones locales en la última década. Documento Ocasional, n° 95, Banco de España.

ANCI - Associazione Nazionale Comuni Italiani (2020). Audizione informale ANCI presso le commissioni bilancio riunite Camera e Senato per la conversione del "DL Rilancio". Available at: https://finanze.regione.emilia-romagna.it/documenti-di-finanza/audizione-anci-dl-34-rilancio-28-05-2020.pdf (Accessed: 14 October 2020).

Ambrosanio, M. F., Balduzzi, P., Bordignon, M. (2016). 'Economic Crisis and Fiscal Federalism in Italy', in: Ahmad, E., Ambrosiano, M., Brosio, G. (Eds.), *Multi-level Finance and the Euro Crisis*, Cheltenham: Edward Elgar, pp. 212–246.

Anessi-Pessina, E., Barbera, C., Langella, C., Manes-Rossi, F., Sancino, A., Sicilia, M., Stec-colini, I. (2020). 'Reconsidering public budgeting after the Covid-19 outbreak: Key lessons and future challenges', *Journal of Public Budgeting, Accounting & Financial Management*, 32(5), pp. 957–965.

Anessi-Pessina, E., Sicilia, M., Steccolini, I. (2012). 'Budgeting and Rebudgeting in Local Governments: Siamese Twins'? *Public Administration Review*, 72(6), pp. 875–884.

ANMP – Associação Nacional dos Municípios Portugueses (2020). *Os municípios no contexto da pandemia Covid-19*, Legislação publicada com relevo para as autarquias locais; Circular No. 33/2020, 18 de Maio.

Arunachalam, M., Chen, C., Davey, H. (2017). 'A model for measuring financial sustainability of local authorities: Model development and application', *Asia-Pacific Management Accounting Journal*, 12(1), pp. 39–76.

Auerbach, Alan J., et al. (2020). 'Effects of COVID-19 on Federal, State, and Local Government Budgets.' *Brookings Papers on Economic Activity*, pp. 229–278.

Australian Bureau of Statistics (ABS) (2021). *ABS's website*. Available at: https://www.abs.gov.au (Accessed: 1 September 2021).

Australian Bureau of Statistics (ABS) (2020). *Wiluna Local Government Area 2016 Quick Stats*. Available at: https://quickstats.censusdata.abs.gov.au/census_services/getproduct/census/2016/quickstat/LGA59250?opendocument (Accessed: 12 August 2021).

Australian Bureau of Statistics (ABS) (2020a). *Brisbane City Local Government Area 2016 Quick Stats*. Available at: https://quickstats.censusdata.abs.gov.au/census_services/getproduct/census/2016/quickstat/LGA31000?opendocument (Accessed: 12 August 2021).

Australian Government (2010). 2009–10 report on the operation of the Local Government (Financial Assistance) Act 1995, Canberra: Department of Regional Australia, Local Government, Arts and Sport.

Australian Local Government Association (ALGA) (2020). *Councils given extra time to find shovel-ready local road projects*. Available at: https://alga.asn.au/councils-given-extra-time-to-find-shovel-ready-local-road-projects/ (Accessed: 12 August 2021).

Australian Local Government Association (ALGA) (2021). *Local Government Key Facts and Figures*. Available at: https://alga.asn.au/facts-and-figures/ (Accessed: 1 September 2021).

Badelt, C. (2021). *Austria's Economic Policy in the Time of Covid-19 and Beyond. An Assessment at the Turn of the Year 2020-21*. No. 1/2021. Reports on Austria. WIFO.

Barbera, C., Guarini, E., Steccolini, I. (2020), 'How do governments cope with austerity? The roles of accounting in shaping governmental financial resilience', *Accounting, Auditing & Accountability Journal*, 33(3), pp. 529–558.

Barbera, C. *et al.* (2017), 'Governmental financial resilience under austerity in Austria, England and Italy: How do local governments cope with financial shocks'? *Public Administration*, 95(3), pp. 670–697.

Barbera, C. *et al.* (2019), 'Local government strategies in the face of shocks and crises: the role of anticipatory capacities and financial vulnerability', *International Review of Administrative Sciences*, 87(1), pp. 154–170, doi: 10.1177/0020852319842661.

Bastida, F., Guillamon, M.D., Benito, B. (2014), 'Explaining interest rates in local government borrowing', *International Public Management Journal*, 17, pp. 45–73.

Bauer, H., Biwald, P. (2019), 'Governance im österreichischen Bundesstaat voranbringen', in: Bauer, H., Biwald, P., Mitterer, K. (Eds.), *Governance-Perspektiven in Österreichs Föderalismus: Herausforderungen Und Optionen*, Öffentliches Management Und Finanzwirtschaft. Wien: NWV, Neuer Wissenschaftlicher Verlag.

Bauer, H., Biwald, P., Mitterer, K. (2017), 'Kritische Analysen und Reformvorschläge zum Finanzausgleich 2008', in: Bauer, H., Biwald, P., Mitterer, K., Thöni, E. (Eds.), *Finanzausgleich 2017: ein Handbuch – mit*

Kommentar zum FAG 2017, Öffentliches Management und Finanzwirtschaft. Wien Graz: NWV Verlag GmbH, pp. 117–140.

Berne, R., Schramm, R. (1986), *The Financial Analysis of Governments*. Englewood Cliffs. NJ, USA: Prentice Hall.

Bespalova, M., Andersen, K. (2013), 'Local and regional democracy in Italy', Council of Europe, CG (24)8, Available at: https://rm.coe.int/168071a5e9 (Accessed: 1 April 2021).

Betsill, M., Bulkeley, H. (2006), 'Cities and the multilevel governance of global climate change', *Global Governance*, 12(2), pp. 141–159.

Bettoni, G. (2017) 'Constitutional Reform and Territorial Organisation in Italy', in: Ruano, J. M., Profirain, M. (Eds.), *Palgrave Handbook of Decentralization*. Palgrave McMillan, pp. 103–122.

Biwald, P., Mitterer, K. (2020). Beitrag der Gemeinden zur Bewältigung der Wirtschafts- und Arbeitsmarktkrise. WISO 43.

Blayney Shire Council (BSC) (2020). Minutes of the Blayney Shire Council Ordinary Meeting Held Via the video Conferencing Platform Zoom, on 18 May 2020. Available at: https://www.blayney.nsw.gov.au/your-council/council-meetings-and-committees/business-papers-and-minutes/business-papers-and-minutes (Accessed: 1 April 2021).

BMF (2020). Durchführungsbestimmungen zum Kommunalinvestitionsgesetz 2020. Richtlinien gemäß § 2 Abs. 3 KIG 2020.

Boin, A., Lodge, M. (2016), 'Designing resilient institutions for transboundary crisis management: a time for public administration', *Public Administration*, 94(2), pp. 289–298.

Bracci, E., Humphrey, C., Moll, J., Steccolini, I. (2015), 'Public sector accounting, accountability and austerity: more than balancing the books', *Accounting, Auditing & Accountability Journal*, 28(6), pp. 878–908.

Brand, S., Steinbrecher, J., Krone, E. (2020), *Kommunalfinanzen in der Corona-Krise: Einbruch erwartet, Investitionen unter Druck*, Frankfurt am Main: KfW Research.

Bröthaler, J., Haindl, A., Mitterer, K. (2017). 'Funktionsweisen und finanzielle Entwicklungen im Finanzausgleichssystem', in: Bauer, H., Biwald, P., Mitterer, K., Thöni, E. (Eds.), *Finanzausgleich 2017: ein Handbuch – mit Kommentar zum FAG 2017, Öffentliches Management und Finanzwirtschaft*. Wien Graz: NWV Verlag GmbH, pp. 79–116.

Brusca, I., Manes Rossi, F., Aversano, N. (2015), 'Drivers for the financial condition of local government: a comparative study between Italy and Spain', *Lex Localis – Journal of Local Self-Government*, 13(2), pp. 161–184.

Cabaleiro, R., Buch, E., Vaamonde, A. (2013), 'Developing a method to assessing the municipal financial health', *The American Review of Public Administration*, 43(6), pp. 729–751.

Camera dei deputati (2018). La disciplina del pareggio di bilancio per regioni ed enti locali.

Capalbo, E., Grossi, G. (2014), 'Assessing the influence of socioeconomic drivers on Italian municipal financial destabilization', *Public Money & Management*, 34(2), pp. 107–114.

Capeci, J. (1994), 'Local fiscal policies, default risk, and municipal borrowing costs', *Journal of Public Economics*, 53(3), pp. 73–89.

Cepiku, D., Mussari, R., Giordano, F. (2016), 'Local governments managing austerity: Approaches, determinants and impact'. *Public Administration*, 94(1), pp. 223–243.

Cepiku, D., Giordano, F. (2021), 'Economic crisis and public administration', *Oxford Research Encyclopedia of Politics.*, Available at: https://oxfordre.com/politics/view/10.1093/acrefore/9780190228637.001.0001/acrefore-9780190228637-e-1435. (Accessed: 25 August 2021).

City of Parramatta (CoP) (2020). *COVID-19: How Council is responding.* Available at: https://www.cityofparramatta.nsw.gov.au/council/covid-19-how-council-is-responding (Accessed: 10 January 2021).

CNEL - Consiglio Nazionale dell'Economia e del Lavoro (2020). Finanza locale: Impatto del Covid-19. Gli impatti della pandemia sulle finanze delle amministrazioni comunali, PAR 254/C19 28.07.2020, Roma.

Coffs Harbour City Council (CHCC) (2020). *Council Assistance Measures COVID-19.* Available at: https://www.coffsharbour.nsw.gov.au/Pages/Council-Assistance-Measures-COVID-19.aspx (Accessed: 2 February 2021).

Cohen, S., Karatzimas, S., Naoum, V.-C. (2017), 'The sticky cost phenomenon at the local government level: Empirical evidence from Greece', *Journal of Applied Accounting Research*, 18(4), pp. 445–463.

Corte dei Conti (2016). Relazione sulla gestione finanziaria degli enti locali. Available at: http://www.corteconti.it/export/sites/portalecdc/_documenti/controllo/sez_autonomie/2016/delibera_8_2016_frg.pdf (Accessed: 3 March 2021).

Corte dei Conti (2018). Andamenti della gestione finanziaria degli Enti locali nel primo anno di applicazione della contabilità armonizzata, Available at: http://www.corteconti.it/export/sites/portalecdc/_documenti/controllo/sez_autonomie/2018/delibera_4_2018.pdf (Accessed: 20 March 2021).

Corte dei Conti (2021). Relazione sulla gestione finanziaria degli enti locali. Available at: https://www.corteconti.it/Download?id=5760a612-e02d-467b-ac5a-5a2b1fbe6a6d (Accessed: 14 September 2021).

Council of Europe (2019), Local and regional democracy in Bosnia and Herzegovina, Congress of local and regional authorities, Report CG 37(2019). Available at https://rm.coe.int/090000168098072a (Accessed: 5 September 2020).

Czypionka, T., Kocher, M. G., Schnabl, A. (2020). *Österreichs Wirtschaft in der Corona-Pandemie. Perspekt. Wirtsch*, 21, pp. 280–289. doi: https://doi.org/10.1515/pwp-2020-0024.

Davies, S. (2011), 'Regional resilience in the 2008-2010 downturn: comparative evidence from European countries', *Cambridge Journal of Regions, Economy and Society*, 4(3), pp. 369–382.

de Jong, M., Ho, A. T. (2020), 'Emerging fiscal health and governance concerns resulting from Covid-19 challenges', *Journal of Public Budgeting, Accounting & Financial Management*, 33(1), pp. 1–11.

Dollery, B. E. (2002), 'A century of vertical fiscal imbalance in Australian federalism', *History of Economics Review*, 36(1), pp. 26–43.

Dollery, B. E., Crase, L., Johnson, A. (2006), *Australian Local Government Economics*. Sydney: UNSW Press.

Dollery, B. E., Wallis, J. L., Allan, P. (2006), 'The debate that had to happen but never did: The changing role of Australian local government', *Australian Journal of Political Science*, 41(4), pp. 553–567.

Downing, R. G. (1991), 'Urban county fiscal stress: A survey of public officials' perceptions and government experiences', *Urban Affairs Quarterly*, 27, pp. 314–325.

European Commission (2019). Country Report Austria 2019. European Commission.

Federal Office of Statistics, Germany (2021). *Countries and regions: Regional statistics.* Available &at: https://www.destatis.de/EN/Themes/Countries-Regions/Regional-Statistics/_node.html (Accessed: 1 September 2021).

Fernandes, M. J. *et al.* (2020), *Anuário financeiro dos municípios portugueses – 2019*; CICF/IPCA e CICP/UM (Eds.), Lisboa: Ordem dos Contabilistas Certificados [ISSN 2182-5564]. Available at https://www.occ.pt/news/Anuarios/afmp2019.pdf (Accessed: 4 February 2021).

Freier, R., Geissler, R. (2020), 'Kommunale Finanzen in der Corona-Krise: Effekte und Reaktionen', *Wirtschaftsdienst*, 5, pp. 356–363.

Geissler, R. (2019), 'Germany', in Geissler, R., Hammerschmid, G., Raffer, C. (Eds.), *Local Public Finance in Europe: Country Mappings*. Berlin and Guetersloh: Hertie School and Bertelsmann Stiftung, pp.102–110.

Geissler, R., Ebinger, F. (2019). 'Austria', in: Geissler, R., Hammerschmid, G., Raffer, C. (Eds.), *Local Public Finance in Europe: Country Reports*. Bertelsmann Stiftung, Hertie School of Governance.

Geissler, R., Hammerschmid, G., Raffer, C. (2019), *Local Public Finance in Europe*. Berlin: Bertelsmann Stiftung.

Geissler, R., Hammerschmid, G., Raffer, C. (Eds.) (2021), *Local Public Finance: An International Comparative Regulatory Perspective*. Switzerland: Springer.

Grossi, G., Cepiku, D. (2014), 'Financial sustainability and cutback management: Global issues for public organizations. Editorial', *Public Money & Management*, 34(2), pp. 79–81.

Grossi, G., Ho, A. T., Joyce, P. G. (2020), 'Budgetary responses to a global pandemic: Inter-national experiences and lessons for a sustainable future', *Journal of Public Budgeting, Accounting & Financial Management*, 32(5), pp. 737–74.

Gunnedah Shire Council (GSC) (2020). *COVID-19 Business Support Package.* Available at: http://gunnedah.nsw.gov.au/images/GunnedahShireCouncil/COUNCIL/KEEP-IN-TOUCH/News-and-Media/COVID-19/COVID19%20Business%20Support%20Package.pdf (Accessed: 20 February 2021).

Henneke, H.-G. (2020), 'Kommunen sind Stabilitätsanker in der Krise', *Der Landkreis*, 4, pp. 146–148.

Hochrainer, S. (2006), *Macroeconomic Risk Management Against Natural Disasters*. Wiesbaden: Deutscher Universitats-Verlag.

Hopper, T. (2020), 'Swimming in a sea of uncertainty – business, governance and the Coronavirus (Covid-19) pandemic', *Journal of Accounting and Organizational Change*, 16(4), pp. 533–539.

Independent Local Government Review Panel (2013). *Revitalizing Local Government*. Sydney: Independent Local Government Review.

Jacob, B., Hendrick, R. (2012), 'Assessing the Financial Condition of Local Governments: What Is Financial Condition and How Is IT Measured', in: Levine, H., Justice, B. J., Scorsone, E. A. (Eds.), *Handbook of Local Government Fiscal Health*. Burlington: Jones & Bartlett Publishers, pp. 11–40.

Joffe, M. (2020), 'Assigned and Unassigned General Fund Balances before the Pandemic', Mercatus Center George Mason University. Policy Brief. Available at: https://www.mercatus.org/publications/urban-economics/assigned-and-un-assigned-general-fund-balances-pandemic. (Accessed: 5 September 2020).

Jorge, S. (2015), 'Autonomia e (In)Dependência Financeira dos Municípios', in: de Sousa, L., Tavares, A. F., da Cruz e Susana Jorge, N. F. (Eds.), *A Reforma do Poder Local em Debate*. Lisboa: ICS – Imprensa de Ciências Sociais, Chapter 14, pp. 145–151.

Jusufbašić, E. (2011), 'Organisation of fiscal policy on BiH level', *Public Law Notebooks*, Foundation Public Law Centre, 2(5), pp. 59–72.

Ku-ring-gai Council (KRGC) (2020). *Ku-ring-gai Council approves COVID-19 assistance package*. Available at: http://www.kmc.nsw.gov.au/Your_Council/Organisation/News_and_media/Latest_news_-_media_releases/Ku-ring-gai_Council_approves_COVID-19_assistance_package (Accessed: 17 June 2021).

Kuhlmann, S., Wollmann, H. (2014), *Introduction to Comparative Public Administration: Administrative Systems and Reforms in Europe*. Cheltenham (UK): Edward Elgar.

Levine, H., Jonathan B., J., Eric Anthony, S. (Eds.) (2012). *Handbook of Local Government Fiscal Health*. Burlington, MA: Jones & Bartlett Publishers.

Lismore City Council (LCC) (2020). *Covid 19 support for businesses*. Available at: https://yoursay.lismore.nsw.gov.au/covid-19-business-support-information (Accessed: 21 June 2021)

Lismore City Council (2020). *New $100, 000 pump track for Nesbitt Park*. Available at: https://www.lismore.nsw.gov.au/cp_themes/news/page.asp?p=DOC-OYP-44-38-00 (Accessed: 21 June 2021)

Local Government Initiative (2018). Local government in Bosnia and Herzegovina: Report on consultations of a joint commission on local government. Available at: http://europa.ba/wp-content/uploads/2018/06/Master-LGI-report-03062018-bhs-web.pdf (Accessed 16 September 2020)

Local Government New South Wales (LGNSW) (2020). Industrial awards. Available at: https://www.lgnsw.org.au/member-services/industrial-awards (Accessed: 22 June 2021).

Local Government New South Wales (LGNSW) (2020a). Councils are helping to ensure communities have access to enough food and other goods. Available at: https://www.lgnsw.org.au/news/media-release/media-release-councils-are-helping-ensure-communities-have-access-enough-food-and (Accessed: 22 June 2021).

Lodge, M., Hood, C. (2012), 'Into an age of multiple austerities? Public management and public service bargains across OECD countries', *Governance*, 25, pp. 79–101.

Maher, C. S., Hoang, T., Hindery, A. (2020), 'Fiscal responses to Covid-19: Evidence from local governments and nonprofits', *Public Administration Review*, 80(4), pp. 644–650.

Martell, C. R. (2008), 'Fiscal institutions of Brazilian municipal borrowing', *Public Administration and Development*, 28, pp. 30–41.

Meneguzzo, M., Sancino, A., Guenon, M., Fiorani, G. (2013), 'New development: The crisis and European local government reforms', *Public Money & Management*, 33(6), pp. 459–462.

McManus, S., Seville, E., Brunsdon, D., Vargo, J. (2007). *Resilience management: A framework for assessing and improving the resilience of organisations. Report for the Resilient Organisations Programme*, New Zealand. Available at: http://cpor.org/ro/ResilienceMgmtResearch(2007).pdf (Accessed: 2 November 2020).

Mikesell, J. L. (2013), *Fiscal Administration*, 8th edn. Belmont, CA: Wadsworth.

Ministarstvo finansija i trezora Bosne i Hercegovine (2019). Information of public debt of Bosnia and Herzegovina on 31.12.2019, Sarajevo March 2019. Available at https://www.mft.gov.ba/bos/images/stories/javni_dug/informacije/2020/april/Informacija%20o%20stanju%20javne%20zaduzenosti%20BiH%20na%20dan%2031%2012%202019%20BOS.pdf (Accessed: 24 September 2020).

Mitterer, K. (2020). Krise der Gemeindefinanzen. ÖGZ – Österr. Gem.-Ztg. 10/2020, pp. 11–12.

Mitterer, K., Biwald, P., Haindl, A. (2016). Länder-Gemeinde-Transferverflechtungen.

Mitterer, K., Biwald, P., Seisenbacher, M. (2021). Österreichische Gemeindefinanzen 2021 – Entwicklungen 2009 bis 2022.

Mitterer, K., Biwald, P., Seisenbacher, M. (2020). Österreichische Gemeindefinanzen 2020 – Entwicklungen 2009 bis 2023.

Mitterer, K., Hochholdinger, N. (2020). Auswirkungen der Corona-Krise auf die Städte. Befragungsergebnisse einer Erhebung im Auftrag des Österreichischen Städtebundes im Zeitraum Mitte-Ende Mai 2020.

Mitterer, K., Prorok, T. (2020). Herausforderungen der Gemeinden im österreichischen Föderalismus, in: Hermann, A.T., Ingruber, D., Perlot, F., Praprotnik, K., Hainzl, C. (Eds.), *Regional, National, Föderal: Zur Beziehung Politischer Ebenen in Österreich*. Wien: Facultas.

Morris, A. (2002). The commonwealth grants commission and horizontal fiscal equalisation. *Australian Economic Review*, 35(3), pp. 318–324.

Mostacci, E. (2016). 'From the ideological neutrality to the neoclassical interpretation: The evolution of the Italian constitutional law of public debt and deficit'. In: *Fiscal Rules – Limits on Governmental Deficits and Debts*. Cham: Springer, pp. 173–204.

Mühlberger, P., Ott, S. (2016). *Die Kommunen im Finanz- und Steuerrecht*. Graz, Wien: dbv-Verlag

Mujakić, M. I. (2013). *Legal Aspects of Financing Local Self-Government in BiH, HKJU-CCPA*, 13(2), pp. 611–623.

NALAS (2020). Survey: Sought-East European Local Governments in post Covid-19 social-economic recovery, Network of Associations of Local Authorities of South East Europe (NALAS).

National Institute of Statistics, Spain (2021). *Instituto Nacional de Estadística*. Available at: https://www.ine.es (Accessed: 1 September 2021).

National League of Cities. Available at: https://www.nlc.org/wp-content/uploads/2020/12/NLC_Survey_November_2020_One_Pager.pdf. (Accessed: 5 December, 2020).

National Statistic Office, Italy (2021). *Censimenti permanenti delle unità economiche - Rilevazione censuaria delle istituzioni pubbliche*. Available at: https://www.istat.it/it/archivio/216271 (Accessed: 1 September 2021).

Nees, M., Scholz, B. (2020), *Kommunalfinanzbericht 2020 Perspektiven der Kommunalfinanzen in Nordrhein-Westfalen: Anforderungen an die Bundes- und Landespolitik*. Düsseldorf: Ver.di NRW.

Nemec, J., Špaček, D. (2020), 'The Covid-19 pandemic and local government finance: Czechia and Slovakia', *Journal of Public Budgeting, Accounting & Financial Management*, 32(5), pp. 837–846.

NSW Government (2020). Regulatory changes to take pressure off ratepayers, businesses and councils. Available at: https://www.nsw.gov.au/news/regulatory-changes-to-take-pressure-off-ratepayers-businesses-and-councils (Accessed: 16 April 2021).

NSW Government (2020a). NSW local government economic stimulus package. Available at: https://www.olg.nsw.gov.au/wp-content/uploads/2020/05/COVID-19-Local-Government-Economic-Stimulus-Package-FAQS-01052020.pdf (Accessed: 16 April 2021).

NSW Government (2020b). Funding boost for NSW council pounds. Available at: https://www.olg.nsw.gov.au/wp-content/uploads/2020/05/MMR-500000-funding-boost-for-council-pounds.pdf (Accessed: 16 April 2021).

NSW Government (2020c). E-Planning enhancements. Available at: https://www.olg.nsw.gov.au/wp-content/uploads/2020/05/MMR-Nearly-10-million-in-enhancements-for-eplanning.pdf (Accessed: 16 April 2021).

OECD (2020a). *The Territorial Impact of Covid-19: Managing the Crisis across Levels of Government*. Paris: OECD Publishing.

OECD (2020b). *OECD Policy Responses to Coronavirus (COVID-19). Cities policy responses. Updated 23 July 2020*, Available at: https://www.oecd.org/coronavirus/policy-responses/cities-policy-responses-fd1053ff/ (Accessed: 2 February 2021).

OECD (2020c). *Covid-19 and fiscal relations across levels of government*, OECD Policy Responses to Coronavirus (Covid-19).

OECD (2021). *OECD Economic Outlook, Volume 2021 Issue 1: Preliminary version, No. 109*. Paris: OECD Publishing, doi: https://doi.org/10.1787/edfbca02-en.

OECD and World Bank (2019). *Fiscal Resilience to Natural Disasters: Lessons from Country Experiences*. Paris: OECD Publishing.

OECD/UCLG (2019). *2019 Report of the World Observatory on Subnational Government Finance and Investment – Country Profiles*. Paris: World Observatory of Subnational Government Finance and Investment (SNG-WOFI).

Office of Local Government (OLG) (2018). *Your council: Timeseries Data*. Available at: https://yourcouncil.nsw.gov.au/data/ (Accessed: 15 April 2021).

Office of Local Government (OLG) (2019). *Australian classification of local governments and group numbers.* Available at: https://yourcouncil.nsw.gov.au/wp-content/uploads/2018/05/Australian-Classification-of-Local-Government-and-OLG-group-numbers.pdf (Accessed: 15 April 2021).

Ongaro, E. (2008), 'Introduction: the reform of public management in France, Greece, Italy, Portugal and Spain', *International Journal of Public Sector Management*, 21(2), pp.101–117.

Padovani, E., Iacuzzi, S. (2021) 'Real-time crisis management: Testing the role of accounting in local governments', *Journal of Accounting and Public Policy*, 40(3), 106854.

Padovani, E., Iacuzzi, S., Jorge, S., Pimentel, L. (2021), 'Municipal financial vulnerability in pandemic crises: a framework of analysis', *Journal of Public Budgeting, Accounting and Financial Management*, 33(4), 387–408.

Padovani, E., Rescigno, L., Ceccatelli, J. (2018), 'Municipal bond debt and sustainability in a non-mature financial market: The case of Italy', *Sustainability*, 10(9), pp.1–25.

Person, C., Geissler, R. (2021), 'Four Decades of Municipal Bailouts in Germany', in: Geissler, R., Hammerschmid, G., Raffer, C. (Eds.), *Local Public Finance. An International Comparative Regulatory Perspective*, Cham: Springer, pp. 227–248.

Persson, T., Tabellini, G. (1996), 'Federal fiscal constitutions: Risk sharing and moral hazard', *Econometrica*, 64(3), pp. 623–646.

Peters, B. G. (2011), 'Governance responses to the fiscal crisis: comparative perspectives', *Public Money & Management*, 31(1), pp.75–80.

Pleschberger, W. (2008), 'Schutz "der kommunalen Finanzen. Zur Bewältigung einer föderalen" Asymmetrie am Beispiel des österreichischen Konsultationsmechanismus (Stabilitätspakts)', in: Heinelt, H., Vetter, A. (Eds.), *Lokale Politikforschung Heute, Stadtforschung Aktuell.* Wiesbaden: VS Verlag für Sozialwissenschaften, pp. 51–77.

Poljašević, J., Grbavac, J., Mikerević, D. (2020), 'Budgetary responses to a global pandemic in Bosnia and Herzegovina', *Journal of Public Budgeting, Accounting and Financial Management*, 32(5), pp. 949–956.

Pollitt, C. (2008), *Time, Policy, Management: Governing with the Past.* Oxford: Oxford University Press.

Pollitt, C., Bouckaert, G. (2017), *Public Management Reform: A Comparative Analysis into the Age of Austerity.* Oxford: Oxford University Press.

Pollner, J. D., Camara, M., Martin, L. (2001), *Honduras. Catastrophe Risk Exposure of Public assets. An Analysis of Financing Instruments for Smoothing Fiscal Volatility.* Washington, DC: World Bank.

Raffer, C., Padovani, E. (2019), 'Italy', in: Geissler, R., Hammerschmid, G., Raffer, C. (Eds.), *Local Public Finance in Europe*, Berlin: Bertelsmann Stiftung, pp. 141–153.

Rauskala, I., Saliterer, I. (2015), 'Public Sector Accounting and Auditing in Austria', in: Brusca, I., Caperchione, E., Cohen, S., Rossi, F.M. (Eds.), *Public Sector Accounting and Auditing in Europe: The Challenge of Harmonization,*

IIAS Series: Governance and Public Management. London: Palgrave Macmillan UK, pp. 12–26. https://doi.org/10.1057/9781137461346_2

Roberts, J. (2020). NSW Premier commits $82m to support council ECEC centres in wake of JobKeeper omission, Available at: https://thesector.com.au/2020/04/12/nsw-premier-commits-82m-to-support-council-ecec-centres-in-wake-of-jobkeeper-omission/ (Accessed: 16 April 2021).

Saliterer, I., Jones, M., Steccolini, I. (2017), 'Introduction', in: Steccolini, I., Jones, M., Saliterer, I. (Eds.), *Governmental Financial Resilience, Public Policy and Governance*, Bingley: Emerald Publishing Limited, pp. 1–16.

Seawright, J., Gerring, J. (2008), 'Case study selection techniques in case study research: a menu of qualitative and quantitative options', *Political Research Quarterly*, 61(2), pp. 294–308.

Skatssoon, J. (2020). Council's rejoice over $1.8 billion cash splash. *Government News.* Available at: https://www.governmentnews.com.au/councils-rejoice-over-1-8-billion-cash-splash/?utm_medium=email&utm_campaign=Newsletter%202652020&utm_content=Newsletter%202652020+Version+B+CID_5e3cd8ac7c0d2a5b30824f1f75f94fbd&utm_source=Campaign%20Monitor&utm_term=Councils%20rejoice%20over%2018%20billion%20cash%20splash (Accessed: 17 April 2021).

Šnjegota, D, Poljašević, J., Čegar, B. (2019), Public Sector Accounting, Auditing and Control in Republic of Srpska; chapter in book.

Vašiček, V., Roje, G. (2019). *Public Sector Accounting, Auditing and Controling South Eastern Europe.* London, UK: Palgrave Macmillan. doi: 10.1007/978-3-030-03353-8.

Spanish Ministry of Finance (2020). Haciendas locales en Cifras. Available at: https://www.hacienda.gob.es/es-ES/CDI/Paginas/SistemasFinanciacionDeuda/InformacionEELLs/HaciendasLocalesencifras.aspx (Accessed: 5 March 2021).

Statistik Austria (2021). *Bevölkerungsstand.* Available at: https://www.statistik.at/web_de/statistiken/menschen_und_gesellschaft/bevoelkerung/volkszaehlungen_registerzaehlungen_abgestimmte_erwerbsstatistik/bevoelkerungsstand/index.html (Accessed: 1 September 2021).

Steccolini, I., Jones, M., Saliterer, I. (2017). 'Conclusion', in: Steccolini, I., Jones, M., Saliterer, I. (Eds.), *Governmental Financial Resilience, Public Policy and Governance*. Bingley: Emerald Publishing Limited, pp. 229–240.

Stewart, K., Smith, P. (2007). 'Immature policy analysis: Building capacity in eight major Canadian cities', in: Dobuzinskis, L., Howlett, M., Laycock, D. (Eds.), *Policy Analysis in Canada: The State of the Art.* Toronto: University of Toronto Press, pp. 265–287.

Tamworth Regional Council (TRC) (2020). *Covid-19 How we are responding.* Available at: https://www.tamworth.nsw.gov.au/about/news/covid-19-how-we-are-responding (Accessed: 17 April 2021).

The Armidale Express (23 May 2020). *$100, 000 Program to kick start Uralla post COVID-19, bushfires and drought.*

UCLG (2019). GOLD V 2019. The *localization* of the Global Agendas. How local action is transforming territories and communities. Fifth Global Report on Decentralization and Local Democracy, Barcelona: UCLG, Available at: https://www.gold.uclg.org/reports/gold-v?qt-reports=0#qt-reports (Accessed: 22 September 2020).

Unicredit (2016). Financing Italy's regional and local governments. Credit Research, Sector Report.

U.S. Census Bureau (2021). Available at: https://www.census.gov/programs-surveys/cog.html (Accessed: 10 January 2021).

Vandelli, L. (2012). 'Local Government in Italy'. in: Moreno, A.-M. (Ed.), *Local Government in the Member States of the European Union: A Comparative Legal Approach*. Spain: INAP, pp. 339–365.

Walker, B. *et al.* (2002). 'Resilience management in social-ecological systems: A working hypothesis for a participatory approach', *Conservation Ecology*, 6(1), Available at: http://www.consecol.org/vol6/iss1/art14/ (Accessed: 19 September 2020).

Waverly Council (WC) (2020). *Waverley Council announces $1 million per month relief package for small businesses*. Available at: https://www.waverley.nsw.gov.au/top_link_pages/news_and_media/council_news/news/corona/waverley_council_announces_$1_million_per_month_relief_package_for_small_businesses (Accessed: 17 April 2021).

Zhao, B., Weiner, J. (2015) *Measuring Municipal Fiscal Disparities in Connecticut*. Federal Reserve Bank of Boston, New England Public Policy Center Research Report 15-1. Available at: https://www.bostonfed.org/publications/new-england-public-policy-center-research-report/2015/measuring-municipal-fiscal-disparities-in-connecticut.aspx (Accessed: 5 July 2021).

Index

Page numbers in **bold** refer to tables and those followed by "n" indicates notes.

health care 31, 91
health services 17, 52–55
Hochrainer, S. 9
hospitals 33, 52–53, 88, 90

income tax 18, 30, 32, 38–40, 51, 60, 69, 87, 89
indirect tax rates 38, 39
infrastructure 16–17, 21, 25, 29, 31, 34, 36, 40–42, 44, 50, 53, 55, 61, 88, 90, 97–98, 106
Intergovernmental Fiscal Relations Act (*Finanzausgleichsgesetz, FAG*) 30
intergovernmental transfers 18–19, 28, 30–31, 45, 87, 89
International Monetary Fund (IMF) 41
IPART report 20
Italy: administrative structure and fiscal rules 58–59; country profile **57**; COVID-19 pandemic impact 58–65; expenditure structure 61–63; financial vulnerability 63–65; local governments 57; revenue structure 59–61

Jusufbašić, E. 39

kindergarten 29, 32–33, 49, 51–53, 55, 61
Ku-ring-gai Council 17, **22**

Länder level 27, 28, 29, 32, 33
LG Grants Commissions 18
Lismore City Council **22**
Local Finance Law 69
Local Government Amendment Bill (2021) 20–21
local governments (LGs) 1; in Australia 16–20, 23, 25, 26; in Austria 29–33, 35; autonomy of 11; in Bosnia and Herzegovina 36–46; budgets of 41, 43; development status and potential 40; financial vulnerability 5, 7, 8, **13–14**; in Germany 47; in Italy 57; NSW government economic stimulus to **24**; in Portugal 67, 69, 74; revenues 39; small business and 23; in Spain 76–84; in United States of America 85–92

local revenue(s) 8–9, 11, 20, 45, 51, 55, 61, 63, 80, 87, 89, 96–97, 100
Local Roads Component (LRC) 18
local tax(es) 11, 31, 49–51, 59–60, 63, 69, 80, 87, 96–98
lockdown 1–3, 11, 32, 35, 45–46, 51, 53, 59, 61–62, 65, 99–100

McManus, S. 7
management: crisis 1, 4; debt 4, 68; financial 59, 85, 100; property 69; waste 16, 58, 90
March (Cure Italy) decree 59, 61
May (Relaunch) decree 59, 61
"Memorandum of Understanding on Specific Economic Policy Conditionality" 68
metropolitan 17, 19–21, 25, 57, 107
Ministry of Finance (MoF) 37, 43, 44
Mitterer, K. 27
Municipal Adjustment Program (FAM) 70
municipal budgets 28–30, 33, 35, 38, 40
municipal fees 20, 39–40
Municipalities' National Association 74
municipal revenue 30, 31, 40, 50, 65, 97
Municipal Social Fund (FSM) 69, 73
municipal tax(es) 30–32, 35, 35n2, 60, 71

NALAS (2020) 45
National Council for Economics and Labour (CNEL) 65
non-tax revenues 39
NSW Council 19, 21
NSW Government 23–25, **24**

Organic Law on Financial Stability and Financial Sustainability (LOEPSF) 78, 82–83

Pollitt, C. 3, 14, 103
Portugal: administrative structure and fiscal rules 68–71; country profile **67**; COVID-19 pandemic impact 72–74; expenditure structure 72–73; financial vulnerability 73–74; local governments 67, 69, 74; revenue structure 71–72

For Product Safety Concerns and Information please contact our EU
representative GPSR@taylorandfrancis.com Taylor & Francis Verlag GmbH,
Kaufingerstraße 24, 80331 München, Germany

Printed and bound by CPI Group (UK) Ltd, Croydon, CR0 4YY
11/04/2025
01844010-0012